How
to
Pray

What the Bible Tells Us About
Genuine, Effective Prayer

Reuben A. Torrey

We love hearing from our readers. Please contact us at www.anekopress.com/questions-comments with any questions, comments, or suggestions.

How to Pray – Reuben A. Torrey

Revised Edition Copyright © 2018

First edition published 1900

Cover Design: J. Martin

eBook and Audiobook Icons: Icons Vector/ Shutterstock, Ganibal/Shutterstock

Editors: Paul Miller and Ruth Zetek

Printed in China

Aneko Press

www.anekopress.com

Aneko Press, Life Sentence Publishing, and our logos are trademarks of

Life Sentence Publishing, Inc.
203 E. Birch Street
P.O. Box 652
Abbotsford, WI 54405

RELIGION / Christian Life / Prayer

Paperback ISBN: 978-1-62245-571-3

eBook ISBN: 978-1-62245-572-0

10 9 8 7 6 5 4 3 2

Available where books are sold

Contents

Chapter 1

The Importance of Prayer

In Ephesians 6:18 we read words that point out the tremendous importance of prayer, with startling and overwhelming force: *praying always with all prayer and supplication in the Spirit and watching in this with all perseverance and supplication for all the saints.*

When we stop to weigh the meaning of these words and take note of the connection in which they are found, the intelligent child of God is driven to say, "I must pray, pray, pray. I must put all my energy and all my heart into prayer. Whatever else I do, I must pray."

The American Standard Version is, if possible, even more forceful: *with all prayer and supplication praying at all seasons in the Spirit, and watching thereunto in all perseverance and supplication for all the saints.*

Note the *alls*: *with all prayer, at all seasons, in all*

perseverance, for all the saints. Note the piling up of strong words: *prayer, supplication, perseverance.* Note once more the strong expression, *watching thereunto,* or more literally, "being sleepless thereunto." Paul realized the natural laziness of man, and especially his natural laziness in prayer. How seldom we pray things through! How often churches and individuals get right up to the verge of a great

> How often churches and individuals get right up to the verge of a great blessing in prayer and just then let go, get drowsy, and quit.

blessing in prayer and just then let go, get drowsy, and quit. I wish these words, "being sleepless unto prayer," would burn into our hearts. I wish the whole verse would burn into our hearts.

But why is this constant, persistent, sleepless, overcoming prayer so needful?

First of all, because there is a devil. He is cunning, he is mighty, he never rests, and he is always plotting the downfall of the children of God; and if the children of God relax in prayer, the devil will succeed in ensnaring them.

This is the thought of the context of our passage of Scripture. Ephesians 6:12 says, *For we wrestle not against flesh and blood, but against principalities, against powers, against the lords of this age, rulers of this darkness, against spiritual wickedness in the heavens.* The next verse states, *Therefore, take unto you the whole armour of God, that ye may be able to withstand in the evil day and stand fast, all the work having been finished.* Then a description follows of the different parts of the Christian's armor, which we are to put on if we want to stand against the devil and his powerful schemes. In verse 18, Paul brings it to a culmination, telling us that to everything else we must add prayer – constant, persistent, untiring, sleepless prayer in the Holy Spirit, or else all that we do will be for nothing.

A second reason for this constant, persistent, sleepless, overcoming prayer is that prayer is God's appointed way for obtaining things, and the main reason for that which we lack in our experience, in our life, and in our work is neglect of prayer.

James brings this out very forcibly in his epistle, where he says that you *have not that which ye desire because ye ask not* (James 4:2). These words contain the reason for the poverty and powerlessness of the average Christian: neglect of prayer.

"Why is it," many Christians ask, "that I make so little progress in my Christian life?"

"Neglect of prayer," God answers. "You *have not that which ye desire because ye ask not.*"

"Why is it," many pastors ask, "that I see so little fruit from my labors?"

Again God answers, "Neglect of prayer. You *have not that which ye desire because ye ask not.*"

"Why is it," many Sunday school teachers ask, "that I see so few converted in my Sunday school class?"

Still God answers, "Neglect of prayer. You *have not that which ye desire because ye ask not.*"

"Why is it," pastors and congregations ask, "that the church of Christ makes so little headway against unbelief, error, sin, and worldliness?"

Once more, we hear God answering, "Neglect of prayer. You *have not that which ye desire because ye ask not.*"

The third reason for this constant, persistent, sleepless, overcoming prayer is that those men, such as the apostle Paul, whom God set forth as a pattern of what He expected Christians to be, regarded prayer as the most important business of their lives.

When the increasing responsibilities of the early church crowded in upon them, they *called the multitude of the disciples unto them and said, It is not right that we should leave the word of God and serve tables; therefore, brethren, seek out among you seven men of whom you bear witness, full of the Holy Spirit and wisdom, whom we may appoint over this business. And we will give ourselves continually to prayer and to the ministry of the word* (Acts 6:2-4).

It is evident from what Paul wrote about praying for churches and individuals that much of his time, strength, and thought were given to prayer (see Romans

1:9; Ephesians 1:15-16; Colossians 1:9; 1 Thessalonians 3:10; 2 Timothy 1:3).

All the mighty men of God outside the Bible have been men of prayer. They have differed from one another in many things, but they have been alike in being men of prayer.

But there is a still weightier reason for this constant, persistent, sleepless, overcoming prayer. It is that prayer occupied a very prominent place and played a very important part in the earthly life of our Lord.

For example, turn to Mark 1:35. We read, *And in the morning, rising up a great while before day, he went out and departed into a solitary place and prayed there.* The preceding day had been a very busy and exciting one, but Jesus shortened the hours of needed sleep so that He might rise early and give Himself to much greatly needed prayer.

Turn to Luke 6:12, where we read, *And it came to pass in those days that he went out into the mountain to pray and continued all night in prayer to God.* Our Savior sometimes found it necessary to spend a whole night in prayer.

The words "pray" and "prayer" are used at least twenty-five times in connection with our Lord in the brief record of His life in the four Gospels, and His praying is mentioned in places where those words are not used. Evidently, Jesus spent much of His time and strength in prayer, and a man or woman who does not spend much time in prayer cannot properly be called a follower of Jesus Christ.

There is another reason for constant, persistent, sleepless, overcoming prayer that seems, if possible, even more forceful than the previous reason, namely, that praying is the most important part of the present ministry of our risen Lord.

Christ's ministry did not close with His death. His atoning work was finished then, but when He arose and ascended to the right hand of the Father, He entered upon other work for us just as important in its place as His atoning work. It cannot be separated from His atoning work. Intercessory prayer, or praying on behalf of others, rests upon His atoning work as its basis, but it is necessary for our complete salvation.

This great present work by which Jesus carries our salvation on to completeness is told about in Hebrews 7:25: *Therefore he is able also to save to the uttermost those that come unto God by him, seeing he ever lives to make intercession for them.* This verse tells us that Jesus is able to save us *to the uttermost* – not merely *from* the uttermost, but *to* the uttermost. He is able to save us unto entire completeness and absolute perfection, because He not only died, but He also *ever lives.* The verse also tells us for what purpose He now lives: *to make intercession* for us – to pray. Praying is the main thing He is doing these days. It is by His prayers that He is saving us.

The same thought is found in Paul's remarkable, triumphant challenge in Romans 8:34: *Who is he that condemns them? Christ, Jesus, is he who died and, even more, he that also rose again, who furthermore is at the right hand of God, who also makes entreaty for us.*

If we are to have fellowship with Jesus Christ in His present work, then we must spend much time in prayer. We must give ourselves to earnest, constant, persistent, sleepless, overcoming prayer. I know of nothing that has so much impressed upon me the sense of the importance of praying at all times and being constantly in prayer as the thought that this is the current main business of my risen Lord. I want to have fellowship with Him, and for that reason I have asked the Father that whatever else He may make me, to make me at all times an intercessor – to make me a man who knows how to pray and who spends much time in prayer.

> If we are to have fellowship with Jesus Christ in His present work, then we must spend much time in prayer.

This ministry of intercession is a glorious and mighty ministry, and we can all have a part in it. The man or woman who cannot get to a prayer meeting at church can still have a part in this ministry of intercession. The woman who cleans offices for a living can have a part; she can offer prayers for the saints, for her pastor, for the unsaved, and for foreign missionaries as she cleans. The hardworking businessman can have a part in it, praying as he hurries from duty to duty or from appointment to appointment. Of course, if we want to maintain this spirit of constant prayer, we must take time – and plenty of it – when we close ourselves up in the secret place alone with God for nothing but prayer.

The sixth reason for constant, persistent, sleepless, overcoming prayer is that prayer is the means that God has appointed for us to receive mercy and obtain grace to help in time of need. Hebrews 4:16 is one of the simplest and sweetest verses in the Bible: *Let us, therefore, come boldly unto the throne of his grace, that we may obtain mercy and find grace to help in time of need.* These words make it very plain that God has appointed a way by which we should seek and obtain mercy and grace. That way is prayer – a bold, confident, outspoken approach to the throne of grace, the most holy place of God's presence, where our sympathizing High Priest, Jesus Christ, has entered in our behalf. *Having, therefore, a great high priest who penetrated the heavens, Jesus the Son of God, let us hold fast this profession of our hope. For we do not have a high priest who cannot sympathize with our weaknesses, but was in all points tempted like as we are, yet without sin* (Hebrews 4:14-15).

Mercy is what we need, and grace is what we must have, or all our life and effort will end in complete failure. Prayer is the way to obtain mercy and grace.

There is infinite grace at our disposal, and we make it ours in reality by prayer. Oh, if we only realized the fullness of God's grace that is ours for the asking – its height and depth and length and breadth – I am sure that we would spend more time in prayer. The extent of our acquiring grace is determined by the extent of our prayers.

Who does not feel that he needs more grace? Then ask for it. Be constant, persistent, and untiring in your asking. God delights to have us often and persistently ask, for it shows our faith in Him, and He is greatly pleased with faith. Because we are not ashamed to ask, He will rise and give us as much as we need. *I say unto you, Though he will not rise and give him because he is his friend, yet because of his importunity, he will rise and give him as many as he needs* (Luke 11:8). Most of us know only little streams of mercy and grace, when we could know rivers of God's mercy and grace overflowing their banks!

> **Because we are not ashamed to ask, He will rise and give us as much as we need.**

The next reason for constant, persistent, sleepless, overcoming prayer is that prayer in the name of Jesus Christ is the way Jesus Christ Himself has appointed for His disciples to obtain fullness of joy.

He states this simply and beautifully in John 16:24: *Until now ye have asked nothing in my name; ask, and ye shall receive, that your joy may be fulfilled.* "Made full" is the way the American Standard Version reads. Who does not want his joy filled full? Well, the way to have it filled full is by praying in the name of Jesus. We all know people whose joy is filled full; indeed, it is just running over, shining from their eyes, bubbling out of their very lips, and running off their fingertips when they shake hands with you. Coming in contact with them is like coming in contact with an electrical machine charged with gladness.

Why is it that true prayer in the name of Christ brings such fullness of joy? In part, because we get what we ask; but that is not the only reason, nor the greatest. The greatest reason is that it makes us realize even more that God is real. When we ask something definite of God and He gives it, how real God becomes! He is right there! It is great to have a God who is real and not merely an idea.

I remember once when I suddenly became seriously sick, all alone in my study. I dropped down on my knees and cried to God for help. Instantly all pain left me. I was perfectly well. It seemed as if God stood right there and had put out His hand and touched me.

The joy of that healing was not as great, though, as the joy of meeting with God. There is no greater joy on earth or in heaven than communion with God, and prayer in the name of Jesus brings us into communion with Him. The psalmist was surely not speaking only of future joy, but also of present joy, when he said, *in thy presence is fullness of joy* (Psalm 16:11). Oh, the unutterable joy of those moments when we really press into the presence of God in prayer!

You might say, "I have never known joy like that in prayer." I might then ask, "Do you set aside enough time for prayer to actually get into God's presence? Do you really give yourself up to true prayer in the time that you do take?"

The eighth reason for constant, persistent, sleepless, overcoming prayer is that prayer, in every care and anxiety and need of life, with thanksgiving, is the means that God has appointed for us to obtain freedom from all anxiety, and the means of the peace of God which passes all understanding.

Be anxious for nothing, Paul says, *but in every thing by prayer and supplication with thanksgiving, let your requests be made known unto God. And the peace of God, which passes all understanding, shall keep your hearts and minds through Christ Jesus* (Philippians 4:6-7). At first glance, this seems to be the picture of a life that is beautiful, but beyond the reach of ordinary humans. That is not true at all.

Verse 6 tells us how the life is attainable by every child of God: *Be anxious for nothing.* The rest of the verse tells us how, and it is very simple: *but in every thing by prayer and supplication with thanksgiving, let your requests be made known unto God.* What could be plainer or simpler than that? Just keep in constant touch with God, and when any trouble or frustration comes up, great or small, speak to Him about it, never forgetting to return thanks for what He has already done. What will the result be? *The peace of God, which passes all understanding, shall keep your hearts and minds through Christ Jesus.*

That is glorious, and it is as simple as it is glorious! I thank God that some are trying it. Don't you know anyone who is always calm and composed? Perhaps he is very agitated and flustered by nature, but troubles, conflicts, changes, and loss now sweep around him, and the peace of God, which passes all understanding, keeps his heart and his thoughts in Christ Jesus.

One night of prayer will save us from many nights of insomnia.

We all know such people as this. How do they manage it? Just by prayer – that is all. Those people who know the deep peace of God, the unfathomable peace that passes all understanding, are always men and women of much prayer.

Some people let the hurry of their lives crowd out prayer, and then they waste much time and energy by constantly worrying. One night of prayer will save us from many nights of insomnia. Time spent in prayer is not wasted, but is time invested at much interest.

The ninth reason for constant, persistent, sleepless, overcoming prayer is that prayer is the method that God Himself has appointed for us to obtain the Holy Spirit.

Upon this point, the Bible is very plain. Jesus says, *If ye then, being evil, know how to give good gifts unto your children, how much more shall your heavenly Father give the Holy Spirit to those that ask him?* (Luke 11:13). Some very good men tell us that we should not pray for the Holy Spirit, but what are they going to do with the plain statement of Jesus Christ, when He asked, *how much more shall your heavenly Father give the Holy Spirit to those that ask him?*

Some years ago, when it was announced that I was going to preach on the baptism of the Holy Spirit, a brother came to me before the sermon and said with much feeling, "Be sure and tell them not to pray for the Holy Spirit."

"I will surely not tell them that," I responded, "for Jesus says, *how much more shall your heavenly Father give the Holy Spirit to those that ask him?*"

"Oh yes," he replied, "but that was before Pentecost."

"What about Acts 4:31? Was that before Pentecost or after?"

"After, of course," he answered.

"Read it," I told him.

> *And when they had prayed, the place was shaken where they were assembled together; and they were all filled with the Holy Spirit, and they spoke the word of God with boldness.*

"What about Acts 8:15? Was that before Pentecost or after?"

"After," he said.

"Please read it."

Who, when they were come down, prayed for them that they might receive the Holy Spirit.

He made no answer. What could he answer? It is as plain as day in the Word of God that before Pentecost and after, the first baptism and the subsequent fillings with the Holy Spirit were received in answer to definite prayer. Experience also teaches this.

Undoubtedly, many have received the Holy Spirit the moment they surrendered to God before there was time to pray, but there are many who know they were filled with the Holy Spirit while they were on their knees or faces before God, alone or in company with others, and who again and again since that time have been filled with the Holy Spirit as they were in the place of prayer! I know this as definitely as I know that my thirst has been quenched while I was drinking water.

Early one morning in the Chicago Avenue Church prayer room, where several hundred people had been praying together for a number of hours, the Holy Spirit fell so obviously and the whole place was so filled with His presence that no one could speak or pray, but sobs of joy filled the place. Men went out of that room to different parts of the country, taking trains that very morning, and reports soon came back of the outpouring of God's Holy Spirit in answer to prayer. Others went out into the city with the blessing of God upon them. This is only one instance among many that might be cited from personal experience.

If we would only spend more time in prayer, there would be more fullness of the Spirit's power in our work. Many, many men who once worked unmistakably in the power of the Holy Spirit are now filling the air with empty shouts and beating the air with meaningless gestures, because they have let prayer be crowded out by other things. We must spend much time on our knees before God if we want to serve Him in the power of the Holy Spirit.

The tenth reason for constant, persistent, sleepless, overcoming prayer is that prayer is the means that Christ has appointed so that our hearts will not become burdened with overindulgence, drunkenness, and the cares of this life, so that the day of Christ's return does not come upon us suddenly when we are not ready.

One of the most interesting and solemn passages about prayer in the Bible tells us this same thing:

> *And take heed to yourselves, lest at any time your hearts be overcharged with excess and drunkenness and cares of this life, and so that day come upon you unawares. For*

> *as a snare it shall come on all those that*
> *dwell on the face of the whole earth. Watch*
> *ye therefore and pray always that ye may be*
> *accounted worthy to escape all these things*
> *that shall come to pass and to stand before*
> *the Son of man.* (Luke 21:34-36)

According to this passage, there is only one way that we can be prepared for the coming of the Lord when He appears, and that is through much prayer. The coming again of Jesus Christ is a subject that is awakening much interest and discussion in our day, but it is one thing to be interested in the Lord's return and to talk about it, and quite another thing to be prepared for it.

We live in an environment that has a constant tendency to cause us to be unprepared for Christ's coming. The world tends to draw us away from God by its pleasures and cares. There is only one way by which we can rise triumphant above these things, and that is by constantly watching unto prayer, or by sleeplessness unto prayer. *Watch* in this passage is the same strong word used in Ephesians 6:18, and *always* is the same strong phrase as "in every season." The person who does not spend much time in prayer, who is not steadfast and constant in prayer, will not be ready for the Lord when He comes. But we may be ready. How? Pray! Pray! Pray!

There is one more reason for constant, persistent,

sleepless, overcoming prayer, and it is a mighty one: because of what prayer accomplishes. Much has really been said about that already, but there is much more that should be added.

Prayer promotes our spiritual growth as almost nothing else does, except for Bible study. True prayer and true Bible study go hand in hand.

It is through prayer that my sin – including my most secret sin – is brought to light. As I kneel before God and pray, *Search me, O God, and know my heart; try me and know my thoughts and see if there be any wicked way in me* (Psalm 139:23-24), God shines the penetrating rays of His light into the innermost places of my heart, bringing my sins into view, of which I was unaware before.

> True prayer and true Bible study go hand in hand.

In answer to prayer, God washes me from my iniquity and cleanses me from my sin. *Wash me thoroughly from my iniquity and cleanse me from my sin* (Psalm 51:2). In answer to prayer, my eyes are opened to behold wondrous things out of God's Word. *Open my eyes, and I shall behold the wonders of thy law* (Psalm 119:18). In answer to prayer, I get wisdom to know God's way and strength to walk in it. *If any of you lacks wisdom, let them ask of God (who gives abundantly to all, and without reproach), and it shall be given them* (James 1:5).

As I meet God in prayer and gaze into His face, I am changed into His own image from glory to glory.

Therefore we all, beholding as in a glass the glory of the Lord with uncovered face, are transformed from glory to glory into the same likeness, even as by the Spirit of the Lord (2 Corinthians 3:18). Each day that I live a life of true prayer, I become a little more like my glorious Lord.

John Welch, son-in-law to John Knox, was one of the most faithful men of prayer this world has ever seen. He considered the day poorly spent in which he did not spend seven or eight hours alone with God in prayer and in the study of His Word. An elderly man speaking of him after his death said, "He was a type of Christ." How did he become so much like his Master? His prayer life explains the mystery.

Prayer brings power into our work. If we want power for any work to which God calls us, whether it is preaching, teaching, bringing others to Jesus, or raising our children, we can get it by earnest prayer.

A woman with a little boy who was downright disobedient once came to me in desperation and asked, "What can I do with him?"

I asked, "Have you ever tried prayer?"

She said that she had prayed for him at times. I asked if she had made his conversion and his behavior a matter of specific, fervent, expectant prayer. She replied that she had not. She began that day, and at once, there was an unmistakable change in the child, and he grew up to be a fine Christian man.

How many Sunday school teachers have taught for

months and years without having seen any real fruit from their labors, and then after having learned the secret of intercession, by earnest pleading with God they have seen their students brought one by one to Christ! How many simple preachers have become mighty men of God by casting away their confidence in their own ability and gifts and giving themselves up to God to wait upon Him for the power that comes from on high!

John Livingstone, a seventeenth-century Scottish pastor, spent a night with some others in prayer to God and religious conversation, and when he preached the next day in the church in the town of Shotts, five hundred people were converted or otherwise experienced some definite movement of God in their lives on that occasion. Prayer and power are inseparable.

Prayer assists in the conversion of others. There are few people converted in this world unless it is in connection with someone's prayers. I used to think that no human being had anything to do with my own conversion, for I was not converted in church or Sunday school or in a personal conversation with anyone. I was awakened in the middle of the night and converted.

As far as I can remember, I did not have the slightest thought of desiring to be converted when I went to bed and fell asleep; but I was awakened in the middle of the night and was converted in less than five minutes. A few minutes before, I was about as near eternal hell-fire as one gets. I had one foot over the brink and was trying to get the other one over. I thought no human being had anything to do with it, but I had forgotten my mother's prayers, and I learned afterward that one of my college classmates had decided to pray for me until I was saved.

Prayer often prevails where everything else fails. How utterly all of Monica's efforts and pleadings failed with her son, Augustine; but her prayers prevailed with God, and the wild youth became Saint Augustine, the mighty man of God. By prayer, the bitterest enemies of the gospel have become its most valiant defenders. By prayer, the worst criminals have become the most devoted sons of God. By prayer, the most disgraceful women have become the purest saints. Oh, the power of prayer to reach down, down, down where hope itself seems vain, and to lift men and women up, up, up into fellowship with and likeness to God. It is simply wonderful! How little we appreciate this marvelous weapon of prayer!

Prayer often prevails where everything else fails.

Prayer brings blessings to the church. The history of the church has always been a history of dreadful difficulties to overcome. The devil hates the church and seeks to block its progress in every way – by false doctrine, division, inward corruption of life, and any other means. But prayer can make a way through everything.

Prayer will root out heresy, clear up misunderstandings,

sweep away jealousies and animosities, wipe out immoralities, and bring in the full surge of God's reviving grace. History abundantly proves this. In the hour of dire danger, when the case of the church, local or universal, has seemed beyond hope, believing men and women have met together and cried out to God – and the answer has come.

It was so in the days of John Knox. It was so in the days of John Wesley and George Whitfield. It was so in the days of Jonathan Edwards and David Brainerd. It was so in the days of Charles Finney. It was so in the days of the great revival of 1857 in this country and of 1859 in Ireland. It was so in the days of the Welsh revivals, and it will be so again in your day and mine.

Satan has assembled his forces. He is attacking with worldliness, with atheism, with false religions, and even with watered-down versions of Christianity. Christians loyal to the great fundamental truths of the gospel are glaring at one another with a devil-sent suspicion. The world, the flesh, and the devil are having their way. It is now a dark day, but *it is time for thee, O LORD, to act; for they have dissipated thy law* (Psalm 119:126). He is getting ready to work, and now He is listening for the voice of prayer. Will He hear it? Will He hear it from you? Will He hear it from the church as a body? I believe He will.

Chapter 2

Praying unto God

We have seen something of the tremendous importance and the resistless power of prayer, and now we come directly to the question of how to pray with power.

In Acts 12, we have the record of a prayer that prevailed with God and brought great results. In the fifth verse of this chapter, the manner and method of this prayer is described in few words:

> *Prayer was made without ceasing of the church unto God for him.* (KJV)

The first thing to notice in this verse is the brief expression *unto God*. The prayer that has power is the prayer that is offered unto God.

But some will ask, "Is not all prayer unto God?" No.

Much of what is called prayer, both public and private, is not unto God. In order for a prayer to really be unto God, there must be a definite and conscious approach to God when we pray. We must have a definite and clear realization that God is bending over us and listening as we pray.

In much of our prayer, there is really only little thought of God. Our mind is taken up with the thought of what we need, and it is not occupied with the thought of the mighty and loving Father from whom we are seeking what we need. Often we are occupied neither with the need nor with the One to whom we are praying, but our mind is wandering here and there throughout the world. There is no power in that sort of prayer, but when we really come into God's presence, when we really meet Him face-to-face in the place of prayer, when we really seek the things that we desire from *Him*, then there is power.

If we want to pray properly, then the first thing we should do is see to it that we really get an audience with God – that we really get into His very presence. Before a word of petition is offered, we should have the definite and clear awareness that we are talking to God, and we should believe that He is listening to our petition and is going to grant the thing that we ask of Him. This is only possible by the Holy Spirit's power, so we should look to the Holy Spirit to really lead us into the presence of God, not being quick to begin praying until He has actually brought us there.

One night a very active Christian man dropped into a little prayer meeting that I was leading. Before we knelt to pray, I said something like the above, telling all the friends to be sure that they were praying properly. I told them that while they were praying they should be sure that they really were in God's presence, that they had thoughts of Him definitely in mind, and that they were more concerned with Him than with their petition. A few days later, I met this same gentleman, and he said that this simple thought was entirely new to him and that it had made prayer an entirely new experience for him. If we want to pray properly, these two little words must sink deep into our hearts: *unto God*.

The second secret of effective praying is found in the same verse, in the words *without ceasing*. In the American Standard Version, *without ceasing* is rendered *earnestly*. Neither rendering gives the full force of the Greek. The word literally means "stretched-out-ed-ly." It is a pictorial word, and it is wonderfully expressive. It represents the soul being stretched or reaching out in earnest and intense desire. "Intensely" would perhaps come as near in translating it as any English word. It is the word used of our Lord in Luke 22:44, where it is said *he prayed more earnestly; and his sweat was as it were great drops of blood falling down to the ground.*

We read in Hebrews 5:7 that *in the days of his flesh,*

[Christ] *offered up prayers and supplications with strong crying and tears.* Paul requests the saints in Rome to *strive* together with him in their prayers. *Now I beseech you, brethren, for the Lord Jesus Christ's sake, and for the love of the Spirit, that ye strive together with me in your prayers to God for me* (Romans 15:30 KJV).

The word translated "strive" means primarily to contend as in athletic games or in a fight. In other words, the prayer that prevails with God is the prayer into which we put our whole soul, stretching out toward God in intense and agonizing desire.

Much of our modern prayer has no power in it because there is no heart in it.

Much of our modern prayer has no power in it because there is no heart in it. We rush into God's presence, run through a string of petitions, jump up, and go out. If someone would ask us an hour later what we prayed for, often we would not know. If we put so little heart into our prayers, we cannot expect God to put much heart into answering them.

We hear much in our day about the "rest" of faith, but there is such a thing as the "fight" of faith in prayer, as well as in effort. Those who want us to think that they have attained to some elevated height of faith and trust because they never know any agony of conflict or of prayer have surely found a different experience than their Lord and the mightiest victors for God throughout Christian history knew, both in effort and in prayer.

When we learn to come to God with an intensity of desire that wrings the soul, then we will know a power in prayer that most of us do not now know.

But how can we attain this earnestness in prayer? We cannot do so by trying to work ourselves up into it. The true method is explained in Romans 8:26: *And likewise also the Spirit helps our weakness; for we know not how to pray as we ought, but the Spirit itself makes entreaty for us with groanings which cannot be uttered.* The earnestness that we work up in the energy of the flesh is a repulsive thing. The earnestness worked in us by the power of the Holy Spirit is pleasing to God. Here again, if we want to pray properly, we must look to the Spirit of God to teach us to pray.

It is in this connection that fasting comes. In Daniel 9:3, we read that Daniel set his face *unto the Lord God, seeking him in prayer and supplication, in fasting and sackcloth, and ashes.* There are those who think that fasting belongs only to the old covenant and the Law, but when we look at Acts 14:23 and Acts 13:2-3, we find that it was practiced by the sincere men of the apostolic day. *And having ordained elders for them in every congregation and having prayed with fasting, they commended them to the Lord on whom they believed* (Acts 14:23). *As they ministered to the Lord and fasted, the Holy Spirit said, Separate me Barnabas and Saul for the work unto which I have called them. And when they had fasted and prayed and laid their hands on them, they released them* (Acts 13:2-3).

If we want to pray with power, we should pray with fasting. This, of course, does not mean that we should fast every time we pray, but there are times of emergency or special crisis in work or in our individual lives when people of downright earnestness will withdraw themselves even from the satisfaction of natural appetites that would be perfectly proper under other circumstances, in order to give themselves up wholly to prayer.

There is a peculiar power in such prayer. Every great crisis in life and work should be met in this way. There is nothing pleasing to God in our giving up things that are pleasant in a purely Pharisaic and legalistic way, but there is power in that downright earnestness and determination to obtain in prayer the things for which we intensely feel our need. This earnestness and determination lead us to put away everything, even things in themselves that may be right and necessary, so that we may set our faces to seek God and obtain blessings from Him.

A third secret of right praying is also found in Acts 12:5. It appears in three words: *of the church* (KJV). There is power in united prayer. Of course, there is power in the prayer of an individual, but there is vastly increased power in united prayer. God delights in the unity of His people and seeks to emphasize it in every way, so He pronounces a special blessing upon united prayer. We read in Matthew 18:19, *if two of you shall agree on earth as touching anything that they shall ask, it shall be done for them of my Father who is in the heavens.*

This unity, however, must be real. The passage just quoted does not say that if two shall agree in asking, but if two shall agree *as touching* anything they ask. Two people might agree to ask for the same thing, yet there might be no real agreement concerning the thing they ask. One might ask it because he really desires it, while the other might ask it simply to please his friend. But where there is real agreement, where the Spirit of God brings two believers into perfect harmony concerning that which they ask of God, where the Spirit lays the same burden on two hearts – in all such prayer there is absolutely irresistible power.

Chapter 3

Praying and Obeying

One of the most significant verses in the Bible on prayer is 1 John 3:22. John says, *and whatsoever we ask, we receive of him because we keep his commandments and do those things that are pleasing in his sight.*

What an astounding statement! John says, in so many words, that everything he asked for he got. How many of us can say that whatever we ask God for we receive? John explains why this was so: *because we keep his commandments and do those things that are pleasing in his sight.*

In other words, the one who expects God to do as he asks Him must on his part do whatever God asks. If we give a listening ear to all of God's commands to us, He will give a listening ear to all our petitions to Him. If, on the other hand, we turn a deaf ear to His precepts,

He will be likely to turn a deaf ear to our prayers. Here we find the secret of much unanswered prayer. We are not listening to God's Word, and therefore, He is not listening to our petitions.

I was once speaking to a woman who had been a professed Christian, but she had given it all up. I asked her why she did not still follow Jesus, and she said that it was because she did not believe the Bible. I asked her why she did not believe the Bible.

"Because I have tried its promises and found them untrue."

"Which promises?"

"The promises about prayer."

"Which promises about prayer?"

"Does it not say in the Bible, 'Whatsoever you ask believing, you shall receive'?"

"It says something nearly like that."

"Well, I asked fully expecting to get, but I did not receive, so the promise failed."

"Was the promise made to you?"

"Why, certainly; it is made to all Christians, is it not?"

"No, God carefully defines who the 'you' is – whose believing prayers He agrees to answer."

I then turned to 1 John 3:22 and read the description of those whose prayers had power with God. "Now," I asked, "were you keeping His commandments and doing those things that are pleasing in His sight?"

She honestly confessed that she was not, and she

soon came to see that the real difficulty was not with God's promises, but with herself. That is the difficulty with many unanswered prayers today – the one who offers it is not obedient.

If we want to have power in prayer, we must be earnest students of His Word to find out what His will is regarding us; and then having found it, we must do it. One unconfessed act of disobedience on our part will shut the ear of God against many petitions.

This verse, though, goes beyond the mere keeping of God's commandments. John tells us that we must *do those things that are pleasing in his sight.* There are many things that would be pleasing to God for us to do that He has not specifically commanded us. A true child is not content with merely doing those things that his father specifically commands him to do. He studies to know his father's will, and if he thinks that there is anything he can do that will please his father, he does it gladly, even though his father has never given him any specific order to do it. So it is with the true child of God. He does not merely ask whether certain things are commanded or forbidden, but he studies to know his Father's will in all things.

There are many Christians today who are doing things that are not pleasing to God, and are leaving things undone that would be pleasing to God. When you speak to them about these things, they will confront you at once with the question, "Is there any command in the Bible not to do this thing?" And if you cannot show them some verse in which the matter in question is plainly forbidden, then they think they are under no obligation whatsoever to give it up; but a true child of God does not demand a specific command.

If we make it our study to find out and do the things that are pleasing to God, He will make it His study to do the things that are pleasing to us. Here again, we find the explanation of much unanswered prayer: we are not making it the study of our lives to know what would please our Father, and so our prayers are not answered.

Take as an illustration some questions that are constantly coming up regarding going to the theater, dancing, and the use of tobacco. If you speak against them, many who are indulging in these things will ask you triumphantly, "Does the Bible say, 'Thou shalt not go to the theater'?" "Does the Bible say, 'Thou shalt not dance'?" "Does the Bible say, 'Thou shalt not smoke'?"

That is not the question. The question should be, "Is our heavenly Father well pleased when He sees one of His children in the theater, at a dance, or smoking?" That is a question for each person to decide for himself, prayerfully, seeking light from the Holy Spirit. Many people ask, "What is the harm in these things?" It is separate from our purpose to go into the general question, but beyond a doubt, there is great harm in many cases, for they rob our prayers of power.

Psalm 145:18 throws a great deal of light on the question of how to pray: *The LORD is near unto all those that call upon him, to all that call upon him in truth*. That little expression *in truth* is worthy of study. If you will take your concordance and go through the Bible,

The prayer that God answers is the prayer that is real.

you will find that this expression means "in reality" or "in sincerity." The prayer that God answers is the prayer that is real – the prayer that asks for something that is sincerely desired.

Much prayer is insincere. People ask for things that they do not want. Many women are praying for the conversion of their husbands who do not really want their husbands to be converted. They think they do, but if they knew what would be involved in the conversion of their husbands, how it would necessitate an entire change in their manner of doing business, and how consequently it would reduce their income and make necessary a complete change in how they live, the real prayer of their hearts would be, if they were to be sincere with God: "O God, do not convert my husband." They do not want their husbands converted if the conversion comes at so great a cost.

Many churches are praying for a revival that do

not really desire a revival. They think they do, for to their minds a revival means an increase of membership, an increase of income, and an increase of reputation among the churches. But if they knew what a real revival meant, what a searching of hearts on the part of professed Christians would be involved, what a radical transformation of individual, domestic, and social life would be brought about, and many other things that would come to pass if the Spirit of God was poured out in reality and power, the real cry of the church would be: "O God, keep us from having a revival."

Many pastors are praying to be filled with the Holy Spirit who do not really desire it. They think they do, for in their minds, to be filled with the Spirit means new joy, new power in preaching the Word, a wider reputation among men, and a larger prominence in the church. But if they understood what is really involved in being filled with the Holy Spirit – how, for example, it would necessarily bring them into hostility with the world and in opposition to unspiritual Christians, how it would cause their names to be spoken of as evil, how it might necessitate their leaving a good and comfortable living and going down to work in the slums, or even in some foreign land – if they understood all this, their prayer would quite likely be: "O God, keep me from being filled with the Holy Spirit."

When we come to the place where we really desire the conversion of friends at any cost, when we really desire the outpouring of the Holy Spirit whatever it may involve, when we really desire to be filled with the Holy Spirit no matter what may happen, and when we desire anything *in truth* and then call upon God for it *in truth*, God is going to hear.

Chapter 4

Praying in the Name of Jesus and According to His Will

I t was a wonderful word about prayer that Jesus spoke to His disciples on the night before His crucifixion: *And whatsoever ye shall ask the Father in my name, that will I do, that the Father may be glorified in the Son. If ye ask any thing in my name, I will do it* (John 14:13-14).

Prayer in the name of Jesus has power with God. God is well pleased with His Son, Jesus Christ. He always hears Him, and He always hears the prayer that is really in His name. There is a fragrance in the name of Jesus that makes every prayer that bears it acceptable to God. But what is it to pray in the name of Jesus?

Many explanations have been attempted that ordinary minds do not understand. There is nothing mystical or mysterious about this expression of praying in the name of Jesus. If you go through the Bible and examine all the passages in which the expressions *in My name* or *in His name* or similar expressions are used, you will find that they mean just about what they do in modern usage.

If I go to a bank and hand in a check with my name signed to it, I ask that bank *in my own name*. If I have money deposited in that bank, the check will be cashed; if not, it will not be cashed. If, however, I go to a bank with somebody else's name signed to the check, I am asking *in his name*, and it does not matter whether I have money in that bank or any bank; if the person whose name is signed to the check has money there, the check will be cashed.

If, for example, I would go to the First National Bank of Chicago and present a check that I had signed for fifty dollars, the bank teller would say to me, "Why, Mr. Torrey, we cannot cash that. You have no money in this bank." But if I would go to the First National Bank with a check for $5,000 made payable to me and signed by one of the large depositors in that bank, they would not ask whether I had money in that bank or in any other bank, but they would honor the check at once.

It is the same way when I go to the bank of heaven – when I go to God in prayer. I have nothing deposited there. I have absolutely no credit there. If I go in my own name, I will get absolutely nothing; but Jesus Christ has unlimited credit in heaven, and He has granted me the privilege of going to the bank with His name on my checks. When I go in His name, my prayers will be honored to any extent.

To pray in the name of Jesus is to pray on the basis not of my credit, but of His. It is to renounce the thought that I have any claims on God at all, and to approach Him on the basis of Christ's claims. Praying in the name of Jesus is not merely adding the phrase, "I ask these things in Jesus' name" to my prayer. I may put that phrase in my prayer and really be resting in my own merit all the time.

On the other hand, I may leave out that phrase, but really be completely resting in the merit of Jesus. When I really do approach God, not on the basis of my merit, but on the basis of Christ's merit, and not on the basis of my goodness, but on the basis of the atoning blood, God will hear me. *Having therefore, brethren, boldness to enter into the sanctuary by the blood of Jesus* (Hebrews 10:19). Much of our modern prayer is ineffective because people approach God imagining that they have some claim upon God whereby He is under obligation to answer their prayers.

> Much of our modern prayer is ineffective because people approach God imagining that they have some claim upon God whereby He is under obligation to answer their prayers.

Years ago, when Mr. Moody was beginning in

Christian work, he visited a town in Illinois. A judge in the town was an unbeliever. This judge's wife asked Mr. Moody to call upon her husband and talk to him about God. Mr. Moody replied, "I cannot talk with your husband. I am only an uneducated young Christian, and your husband has been educated as an unbeliever."

The wife insisted and would not take no for an answer, so Mr. Moody made the call. The clerks in the outer office quietly laughed as the young salesman from Chicago went in to talk with the scholarly judge. The conversation was short. Mr. Moody said, "Judge, I can't talk with you. You have learned much and are educated in being an unbeliever, and I have no learning; but I simply want to say that if you are ever converted, I want you to let me know."

The judge replied, "Yes, young man; if I am ever converted, I will let you know. Yes, I will let you know."

The conversation ended. The clerks laughed louder when the zealous young Christian left the office, but the judge was converted within a year. Mr. Moody, visiting the town again, asked the judge to explain how it came about.

The judge said, "One night, when my wife was at prayer meeting, I began to grow very uneasy and miserable. I did not know what was wrong with me, but I finally went to bed before my wife came home. I could not sleep all that night. I got up early, told my wife that I did not want any breakfast, and went down to the office. I told the clerks they could take the day off, and I shut myself up in the inner office. I kept growing more and more miserable, and finally I got down and asked God to forgive my sins; but I would not say 'for Jesus' sake,' for I was a Unitarian and I did not believe in the atonement. I kept praying, 'God, forgive my sins,' but no answer came. At last, in desperation I cried, 'O God, for Christ's sake, forgive my sins,' and I found peace at once."

The judge had no access to God until he came in the name of Jesus, but when he came in His name, he was heard and answered at once.

Much light is thrown upon the subject of how to pray by 1 John 5:14-15: *And this is the confidence that we have in God, that, if we ask any thing according to his will, he hears us: And if we know that he hears us in whatever we ask, we also know that we have the petitions that we asked of him.* This passage teaches us plainly that if we are to pray properly, we must pray according to God's will; and if we do, we will without doubt get what we ask of Him.

But can we know the will of God? Can we know that any specific prayer is according to His will? We most surely can. How?

First, by the Word. God has revealed His will in His Word. When anything is definitely promised in the Word of God, we know that it is His will to give that thing. If when I pray, I can find some definite promise of God's Word and lay that promise before God, then I know that He hears me, and if I know that He hears me, then I know that I have the petition that I have asked of Him.

For example, when I pray for wisdom, I know that it is the will of God to give me wisdom, for He says so in James 1:5: *And if any of you lacks wisdom, let them ask of God (who gives abundantly to all, and without reproach), and it shall be given them.* So when I ask for wisdom, I know that the prayer is heard, and I know that wisdom will be given to me. In the same way, when I pray for the Holy Spirit, I know from Luke 11:13 that it is God's will that my prayer is heard and that I have the petition that I have asked of Him: *If ye then, being evil, know how to give good gifts unto your children, how much more shall your heavenly Father give the Holy Spirit to those that ask him?*

Some years ago, a minister came to me at the close of a sermon on prayer at a YMCA Bible school. He said, "You have produced upon those young men the impression that they can ask for definite things and get the very things that they ask." I replied that I did not know whether that was the impression that I produced or not, but that was certainly the impression that I desired to produce.

"But," he replied, "that is not right. We cannot be sure, for we don't know God's will."

I turned at once to James 1:5, read it, and said to

him, "Is it not God's will to give us wisdom, and if you ask for wisdom, do you not know that you are going to get it?"

"Ah!" he said. "We don't know what wisdom is."

I said, "No, for if we did, we wouldn't need to ask; but whatever wisdom is, don't you know that you will get it?"

Certainly it is our privilege to know. When we have a specific promise in the Word of God, if we doubt that it is God's will, or if we doubt that God will do the thing that we ask, we make God a liar.

Here is one of the greatest secrets of prevailing prayer: to study the Word to find what God's will is as revealed there in the promises, and then simply to take these promises and spread them out before God in prayer with the absolutely unwavering expectation that He will do what He has promised in His Word.

There is still another way that we can know the will of God, and that is by the teaching of His Holy Spirit. There are many things that we need from God that are not covered by any specific promise, but we are not left in ignorance of the will of God even then. Romans 8:26-27 says, *And likewise also the Spirit helps our weakness; for we know not how to pray as we ought, but the Spirit itself makes entreaty for us with groanings which cannot be uttered. But he that searches the hearts knows what is the desire of the Spirit, that according to the will of God, he makes entreaty for the saints.*

Here we are distinctly told that the Spirit of God prays in us and draws out our prayer according to God's will. When we are led by the Holy Spirit in any direction to pray for any specific purpose, we may do it in all confidence that it is God's will and that we will get the very thing we ask of Him, even though there might be no specific promise to cover the case. God, by His Spirit, often lays upon us a heavy burden of prayer for some specific individual. We cannot rest, but we pray for him *with groanings which cannot be uttered*. Perhaps the man is entirely beyond our reach, but God hears the prayer, and in many cases, it is not long before we hear of his definite conversion.

The passage of 1 John 5:14-15 is one of the most abused passages in the Bible: *And this is the confidence that we have in God, that, if we ask any thing according to his will, he hears us: And if we know that he hears us in whatever we ask, we also know that we have the petitions that we asked of him.*

The Holy Spirit, beyond a doubt, put these verses into the Bible to encourage our faith. The passage begins with, *This is the confidence that we have in God*, and it closes with, *we also know that we have the petitions that we asked of him*; but one of the most frequent uses of this passage, which was so clearly given to give us confidence, is to introduce an element of uncertainty into our prayers.

Oftentimes when one grows confident in prayer,

some cautious brother will come and say, "Now, don't be too confident. If it is God's will, He will do it. You should add, 'If it is Your will.'"

Certainly there are many times when we don't know the will of God, and all prayer should have as its foundation submission to the excellent will of God; but when we know God's will, we do not need any "ifs." This passage was not put into the Bible so that we would introduce "ifs" into all our prayers, but so that we might discard our "ifs" and have *confidence* and *know that we have the petitions that we asked of Him.*

Chapter 5

Praying in the Spirit

Over and over again, in what has already been said, we have seen our dependence upon the Holy Spirit in prayer. This comes out very definitely in Ephesians 6:18: *praying always with all prayer and supplication in the Spirit*, and in Jude 20: *praying in the Holy Spirit*. Indeed, the whole secret of prayer is found in these three words: *in the Spirit*. God the Father answers the prayer that God the Holy Spirit inspires.

The disciples did not know how to pray as they should, so they came to Jesus and said, *Lord, teach us to pray* (Luke 11:1). We do not know how to pray as we should, but we have another Teacher and Guide nearby to help us. *I will ask the Father, and he shall give you another Comforter, that he may abide with you for ever, even the Spirit of truth, whom the world cannot receive because it does not see him, or know him; but ye know him, for he dwells with you and shall be in you* (John 14:16-17). *The Spirit helps our weakness* (Romans 8:26). He teaches us how to pray.

True prayer is prayer in the Spirit. True prayer is prayer that the Holy Spirit inspires and directs. When

True prayer is prayer that the Holy Spirit inspires and directs.

we come into God's presence, we should recognize our weakness and our ignorance of what we should pray for and how we should pray for it. In the awareness of our utter inability to pray properly, we should look to the Holy Spirit, casting ourselves utterly upon Him to direct our prayers, to lead our desires, and to guide the words of our prayers.

Nothing can be more foolish in prayer than to rush thoughtlessly into God's presence and ask the first thing that comes into our mind, or to quickly ask something that some thoughtless friend has asked us to pray for. When we first come into God's presence, we should be silent before Him. We should look to Him so that His Holy Spirit would teach us how to pray. We must wait for the Holy Spirit and surrender ourselves to the Spirit, and then we will pray in the right way.

Often when we come to God in prayer, we do not feel like praying. What should we do in such a situation? Should we stop praying until we feel like it? Not at all. The time when we most need to pray is when we least feel like praying. We should wait quietly before God and tell Him how cold and prayerless our hearts are. We should look up to Him and trust Him and expect the Holy Spirit to warm our hearts and draw them out in prayer.

It will not be long before the glow of the Spirit's presence will fill our hearts and we will begin to pray with freedom, directness, earnestness, and power. Many of the most blessed times of prayer I have ever known have begun with a feeling of utter deadness and prayerlessness; but in my helplessness and cold-ness I have cast myself upon God and looked to Him to send His Holy Spirit to teach me to pray, and He has done it. When we pray in the Spirit, we will pray for the right things in the right way. There will be joy and power in our prayer.

If we are to pray with power, we must pray with faith. In Mark 11:24, Jesus says, *Therefore I say unto you that everything that ye ask for, praying, believe that ye receive it, and it shall come upon you.* No matter how positive any promise of God's Word may be, we will not enjoy it in actual experience unless we confidently expect its fulfillment in answer to our prayer.

If any of you lacks wisdom, says James, *let them ask of God (who gives abundantly to all, and without reproach), and it shall be given them.* That promise is as positive as a promise can be, but the next verses add, *But ask in faith, not doubting anything. For he that doubts is like the wave of the sea which is driven of the wind and is tossed from one side to another. For let not such a man think that he shall receive anything of the Lord* (James 1:6-7).

There must then be confident, unwavering expectation. There is a faith that goes beyond expectation and believes that the prayer is heard and that the promise is granted. This is seen in Mark 11:24: *Therefore I say unto you that everything that ye ask for, praying, believe that ye receive it, and it shall come upon you.* Some versions properly translate this as *believe that you have received it.*

But how can we get this faith? Let us say with all emphasis that we cannot produce this faith on our own by trying to convince ourselves that we have it. Many people read this promise about the prayer of faith and then ask for things they desire, trying to make themselves believe that God has heard the prayer. This ends only in disappointment, for it is not real faith, and the thing is not granted. It is at this point that many people have a breakdown of faith altogether by trying to work up faith by an effort of their will, and since the thing they made themselves believe they expected to get is not given, the very foundation of their faith is often weakened.

But how does real faith come? Romans 10:17 answers the question: *So then faith comes by hearing, and the ear to hear by the word of God.* If we are to have real faith, we must study the Word of God and find out what is promised, and then simply believe the promises of God. Faith must have a guarantee. Trying to believe something that you want to believe is not faith. Believing what God says in His Word is faith.

If I am to have faith when I pray, I must find some promise in the Word of God on which to rest my faith. Furthermore, faith comes through the Spirit. The Spirit knows the will of God, and if I pray in the Spirit and look to the Spirit to teach me God's will, He will lead me out in prayer according to that will, and He will give me faith that the prayer is to be answered; but in no instance does real faith come by simply deciding that you are going to get the thing that you want to get.

If there is no promise in the Word of God and no clear leading of the Spirit, there can be no real faith, and we should not rebuke ourselves for lack of faith in such a case. But if the thing desired is promised in the Word of God, we may well rebuke ourselves for lack of faith if we doubt, for we are making God a liar by doubting His Word.

Chapter 6

Always Praying and Not Fainting

In two parables in the Gospel of Luke, Jesus teaches the lesson with great emphasis that people should always pray and not grow weary in prayer. The first parable is found in Luke 11:5-8, and the other in Luke 18:1-8.

> *And he said unto them, Which of you shall*
> *have a friend and shall go unto him at*
> *midnight and say unto him, Friend, lend*
> *me three loaves; for a friend of mine in his*
> *journey is come to me, and I have nothing*
> *to set before him? And he from within shall*
> *answer and say, Trouble me not; the door is*
> *now shut, and my children are with me in*

*bed; I cannot rise and give thee. I say unto
you, Though he will not rise and give him
because he is his friend, yet because of his
importunity, he will rise and give him as
many as he needs.* (Luke 11:5-8)

*And he spoke a parable unto them to this
end, that it behooves us always to pray
and not faint, saying, There was in a city
a judge who did not fear God nor regard
man; and there was a widow in that city,
and she came unto him, saying, Defend me
from my adversary. And he would not for a
while, but afterward he said within himself,
Though I do not fear God, nor regard man,
yet because this widow troubles me, I will
do her justice, lest by her continual coming
she weary me.*

*And the Lord said, Hear what the unjust
judge says. And shall not God avenge his
own elect who cry day and night unto him
though he bears long regarding them? I
tell you that he will avenge them speedily.
Nevertheless when the Son of man comes,
shall he find faith on the earth?* (Luke 18:1-8)

In the first of these two parables, Jesus sets forth the
necessity of *importunity* in prayer in a startling way.

The word rendered *importunity* literally means "shame-lessness," as if Jesus wants us to understand that God wants us to draw near to Him with a determination to obtain the things we seek that will not be put to shame by any seeming refusal or delay on God's part. God delights in the holy boldness that will not take no for an answer. It is an expression of great faith, and nothing pleases God more than faith.

Jesus seemed to put the Syrophoenician woman away almost with rudeness, but she would not be put away, and Jesus looked upon her shameless importunity with respect. He said, *O woman, great is thy faith; be it unto thee even as thou desire* (Matthew 15:28). God does not always give us what we ask in answer to our first time of praying about something. He wants to train us and make us strong men and women of prayer by pushing us to work and pray hard for the best things. He makes us "pray through."

> He wants to train us and make us strong men and women of prayer by pushing us to work and pray hard for the best things.

I am glad that this is so. There is no more blessed training in prayer than that which comes through being compelled to ask again and again and again, even through a long period of years, before one obtains that which he seeks from God. Many people call it submission to the will of God when God does not grant them their request the first or second time that they ask, and they say, "Well, perhaps it is not God's will." In general, this is not submission, but spiritual laziness.

We do not call it submission to the will of God when we give up after one or two attempts to obtain things by our own efforts; we call it lack of strength of character. When the strong man of action starts out to accomplish something, if he does not accomplish it the first or second or one-hundredth time, he keeps hammering away until he does accomplish it; and the strong person of prayer, when he starts to pray for something, keeps on praying until he prays it through and obtains what he seeks.

We should be careful about what we ask from God, but when we do begin to pray for something, we should never give up praying for it until we get it, or until God makes it very clear and very definite to us that it is not His will to give it.

Some people want us to believe that it shows unbelief to pray twice for the same thing, and that we ought to accept it by faith the first time that we ask. Undoubtedly there are times when we are able through faith in the Word or the leading of the Holy Spirit to claim the first time that which we have asked of God; but beyond question, there are other times when we must pray again and again and again for the same thing before we get our answer.

Those who will not pray twice for the same thing have gotten beyond their Master. *He went away again and prayed the third time, saying the same words* (Matthew 26:44). George Müller prayed for two men daily for more than sixty years. One of these men was converted shortly before his death – I think at the last service that George Müller held. The other man was converted within a year after his death. One of the great needs of the present day is men and women who will not only start out to pray for things, but who will pray on and on and on until they obtain that which they seek from the Lord.

Chapter 7

Abiding in Christ

*I*f ye abide in me and my words abide in you, ye shall ask what ye will, and it shall be done unto you (John 15:7). The whole secret of prayer is found in these words of our Lord. Here is prayer that has limitless power: *ask what ye will, and it shall be done unto you.*

There is a way of asking for and getting precisely what we ask, and getting all that we ask. Christ gives two conditions of this all-prevailing prayer.

The first condition is *If ye abide in me.* What is it to abide in Christ? Some explanations that have been given of this are so mysterious or complex that to many simpleminded children of God they mean practically nothing at all; but what Jesus meant was really very simple. He was comparing Himself to a vine, and He was comparing His disciples to the branches in the vine.

Some branches continued in the vine; that is, they remained in living union with the vine, so the sap or life of the vine constantly flowed into these branches. They had no independent life of their own. Everything in them was simply the outcome of the life of the vine flowing into them. Their buds, leaves, blossoms, and fruit were not really theirs, but were the buds, leaves, blossoms, and fruit of the vine.

Other branches were completely severed from the vine, or else the flow of the sap or life of the vine into them was in some way hindered. For us to abide in Christ means to have the same relationship to Jesus that the first type of branches has to the vine. To abide in Christ is to renounce any independent life of our own. We must give up trying to think our thoughts, form our resolutions, or cultivate our feelings, but we must simply and constantly look to Jesus to think His thoughts in us, to form His purposes in us, and to feel His emotions and affections in us. It is to renounce all life independent of Christ, and to constantly look to Him for the inflow of His life into us, and the outworking of His life through us. When we do this, and to the extent that we do this, our prayers will obtain that which we seek from God.

This must necessarily be so, for our desires will not be our own desires, but Christ's, and our prayers will not in reality be our own prayers, but Christ praying in us. Such prayers will always be in harmony with God's will, and the Father always hears His Son. When our prayers fail, it is because they are indeed *our* prayers. We have conceived the desire and framed the petition ourselves instead of looking to Christ to pray through us.

To say that we should be abiding in Christ in all our prayers and looking to Christ to pray through Him rather than praying ourselves, is simply another way of saying that we should pray "in the Spirit." When we truly abide in Christ, our thoughts are not our own thoughts, but His; our joys are not our own joys, but His; our fruit is not our own fruit, but His – just as the buds, leaves, blossoms, and fruit of the branch that abides in the vine are not the buds, leaves, blossoms, and fruit of the branch, but of the vine itself, whose life is flowing into the branch and manifests itself in these buds, leaves, blossoms, and fruit.

> When we truly abide in Christ, our thoughts are not our own thoughts, but His.

To abide in Christ, we must, of course, already be in Christ through the acceptance of Jesus as an atoning Savior from the guilt of sin, a risen Savior from the power of sin, and a Lord and Master over all our life. Being in Christ, all that we have to do to abide (or continue) in Christ is simply to renounce our self-life – utterly renouncing every thought, every purpose, every desire, and every affection of our own, and just looking day by day and hour by hour for Jesus Christ to form His thoughts, purposes, affections, and desires in us. Abiding in Christ is really a very simple matter, although it is a wonderful life of privilege and of power.

There is another condition stated in this verse, though it is really connected to the first condition: *and my words abide in you.* If we are to obtain from God all that we ask from Him, Christ's words must abide or continue in us. We must study and adequately devour His words, letting them sink into our thoughts and into our hearts, keeping them in our memory, obeying them constantly in our lives, and letting them shape and mold our daily lives and our every action.

This is really the method of abiding in Christ. It is through His words that Jesus imparts Himself to us. The words He speaks unto us are spirit and life. *The Spirit is he that gives life; the flesh profits nothing; the words that I have spoken unto you, they are Spirit and they are life* (John 6:63).

It is useless to expect power in prayer unless we meditate much upon the words of Christ and let them sink deep and find a permanent residence in our hearts. There are many people who wonder why they are so powerless in prayer, but the very simple explanation of it all is found in their neglect of the words of Christ. They have not hidden His words in their hearts. His words do not abide in them.

It is not by periods of mystical meditation and emotional experiences that we learn to abide in Christ, but it is by feeding upon His Word – His written words as found in the Bible – and looking to the Holy Spirit to implant these words in our hearts and make them alive in us. If we let the words of Christ abide in us in this way, they will stir us up to prayer. They will be the mold in which our prayers are shaped. Our prayers will necessarily be according to God's will, and they will prevail with Him. Prevailing prayer is almost an impossibility where there is neglect of the study of the Word of God.

> **Prevailing prayer is almost an impossibility where there is neglect of the study of the Word of God.**

Mere intellectual study of the Word of God is not enough; we must meditate upon it. The Word of God must be revolved over and over and over in our minds, while we constantly look to God by His Spirit to make that Word a living thing in our hearts. The prayer that is born out of meditation upon the Word of God is the prayer that soars upward most easily to God's listening ear.

George Müller, one of the mightiest men of prayer in recent times, would begin his times of prayer by reading and meditating upon God's Word, until out of the study of the Word a prayer would begin to form itself in his heart. Thus, God Himself was the real author of the prayer, and God answered the prayers which He Himself had inspired.

The Word of God is the instrument through which the Holy Spirit works. It is the sword of the Spirit in more senses than one. The person who wants to know the work of the Holy Spirit in any direction must feed upon the Word. The person who wants to pray in the Spirit must meditate much upon the Word so the Holy Spirit can have something through which He can work. The Holy Spirit works His prayers in us through the Word, and neglect of the Word makes praying in the Holy Spirit an impossibility. If we would feed the fire of our prayers with the fuel of God's Word, all our difficulties in prayer would disappear.

Chapter 8

Praying with Thanksgiving

There are two words often overlooked in the lesson about prayer that Paul gives us in Philippians 4:6-7: *Be anxious for nothing, but in every thing by prayer and supplication with thanksgiving, let your requests be made known unto God. And the peace of God, which passes all understanding, shall keep your hearts and minds through Christ Jesus.* The two important words often overlooked are *with thanksgiving.*

In approaching God to ask for new blessings, we should never forget to return thanks for blessings already granted. If any of us would stop and think about how many of the prayers we have offered to God have been answered, and how seldom we have gone back to God to return thanks for the answers given, I'm sure we would be overwhelmed with remorse. We should be just as direct in giving thanks as we are in prayer. We come to God with very specific needs and requests, but when we give thanks to Him, our thanksgiving is vague and general.

Undoubtedly, one reason why so many of our prayers lack power is because we have neglected to thank God for blessings already received. If anyone were to constantly come to us and ask us for help but would never thank us for helping them, we would soon get tired of helping someone so ungrateful. Indeed, we would soon stop helping them, if only to discourage such ingratitude. Undoubtedly, our heavenly Father, out of a wise regard for our own well-being, often refuses to answer petitions that we send up to Him so that we might be brought to a sense of our ingratitude and be taught to be thankful.

> Undoubtedly, one reason why so many of our prayers lack power is because we have neglected to thank God for blessings already received.

God is deeply grieved by the thanklessness and ingratitude of which so many of us are guilty. When Jesus healed the ten lepers and only one came back to give Him thanks, in wonderment and pain He exclaimed, *Were there not ten cleansed? but where are the nine?* (Luke 17:17). How often He must look down upon us in sadness at how often we forget His repeated blessings and His frequent answers to our prayers!

Returning thanks for blessings already received

increases our faith and enables us to approach God with new boldness and new assurance. Undoubtedly, the reason so many have so little faith when they pray is because they take so little time to meditate upon and thank God for blessings already received. As we meditate upon the answers to prayers already granted, our faith grows bolder and bolder, and we come to feel in the very depths of our souls that there is nothing too difficult for the Lord. As we reflect on the one hand upon the wondrous goodness of God toward us, and on the other hand upon the little thought, strength, and time we put into thanksgiving, we may well humble ourselves before God and confess our sin.

The mighty men and women of prayer in the Bible, and the mighty men and women of prayer throughout the ages of the church's history, have been men and women who were much given to thanksgiving and praise. David was a mighty man of prayer, and his psalms abound with thanksgiving and praise. The apostles were mighty men of prayer, and we read that they *were continually in the temple, praising and blessing God* (Luke 24:53). Paul was a mighty man of prayer, and often in his epistles he breaks out in specific thanksgiving to God for specific blessings and specific answers to prayers.

Jesus is our model in prayer as in everything else. We find in the study of His life that His manner of returning thanks at the simplest meal was so noticeable that two of His disciples recognized Him by this after His resurrection. *And it came to pass as he sat at the table with them, he took bread and blessed it and broke and gave to them. And their eyes were opened, and they knew him* (Luke 24:30-31).

Thanksgiving is one of the inevitable results of being filled with the Holy Spirit, and one who does not learn to give thanks in everything (see 1 Thessalonians 5:18) cannot continue to pray in the Spirit. If we want to learn to pray with power, we would do well to let these two words sink deep into our hearts: *with thanksgiving.*

Chapter 9

Hindrances to Prayer

We have looked very carefully into the positive conditions of prevailing prayer, but there are some things that hinder prayer. God has made these things very plain in His Word.

We find the first hindrance to prayer in James 4:3: *Ye ask and receive not because ye ask amiss, that ye may consume it upon your pleasures.*

A selfish motive in prayer robs prayer of power. Many prayers are selfish. These may be prayers for things for which it is perfectly proper to ask, and for which it is the will of God to give; but the motive of the prayer is entirely wrong, and so the prayer falls powerless to the ground. The true purpose in prayer is that God may be glorified in the answer. If we make any petition simply so we can receive something to use for our own pleasure or in our own gratification in one way or another, we *ask amiss* and should not expect to receive what we ask. This explains why many prayers remain unanswered.

For example, many women pray for the conversion of their husbands. That certainly is a most proper thing to ask; but if a woman's motive in asking for the conversion of her husband is selfish, then it is entirely improper. She might desire that her husband be converted because it would be so much more pleasant for her to have a husband who encourages her in her Christian walk. She might pray for her husband's salvation because it is painful for her to think that her husband might die and be lost forever. For some such selfish reason as this, she desires to have her husband converted. The prayer is purely selfish.

Why should a woman desire the conversion of her husband? First of all and above all, she should desire her husband's conversion so that God may be glorified, because she cannot bear the thought that God the Father should be dishonored by her husband trampling underfoot the Son of God. The wife might benefit from her husband's conversion and be glad that he would be in heaven for eternity, but if she neglects the main reason – the glory of God – then she is missing the heart of prayer.

Many people pray for revival. This certainly is a prayer that is pleasing to God, and it is in line with His will; but many prayers for revivals are purely selfish. The churches desire revivals in order that the membership may be increased, in order that the churches may have a position of more power and influence in the community, in order that the churches' treasuries may be filled, or in order that a good report may be made at the annual conference. For such inferior purposes as these, churches and pastors often pray for revival, and often too, God does not answer the prayer.

Why should we pray for revival? We should pray for revival for the glory of God, because we cannot endure it that God should continue to be dishonored by the worldliness of the church, by the sins of unbelievers, and by the proud unbelief of the day. We should pray for revival because God's Word is being made void, and in order that God may be glorified by the outpouring of His Spirit on the church of Christ. For these reasons first of all and above all, we should pray for revival.

Many prayers for the Holy Spirit are purely selfish prayers. It certainly is God's will to give the Holy Spirit to those who ask Him; He has told us so plainly in His Word. *If ye then, being evil, know how to give good gifts unto your children, how much more shall your heavenly Father give the Holy Spirit to those that ask him?* (Luke 11:13). However, many prayers for the Holy Spirit are hindered by the selfishness of the motive that lies behind the prayer.

Men and women pray for the Holy Spirit in order

that they may be happy, or that they may be saved from the wretchedness of defeat in their lives, or that they may have power as Christian workers, or for some other purely selfish motive. Why should we pray for the Spirit? In order that God may no longer be dishonored by the low level of our Christian lives and by our ineffectiveness in service, and in order that God may be glorified in the new beauty that comes into our lives and the new power that comes into our service.

The second hindrance to prayer is found in Isaiah 59:1-2: *Behold, the LORD's hand is not shortened, that it cannot save; nor his ear heavy, that it cannot hear: But your iniquities have separated between you and your God, and your sins have hid his face from you, that he will not hear.* Sin hinders prayer. Many people pray and pray and pray, but get absolutely no answer to their prayer. Perhaps they are tempted to think that it is not the will of God to answer, or they may think that the days when God answered prayer, if He ever did, are over.

This is what the Israelites seemed to have thought. They thought that the Lord's hand was shortened, that it could not save, and that His ear could no longer hear. "Not so," said Isaiah. "God's ear is just as open to hear as ever. His hand is just as mighty to save, but there is a hindrance. That hindrance is your own sins." *Behold, the LORD's hand is not shortened, that it cannot save; nor his ear heavy, that it cannot hear: But your iniquities have separated between you and your God, and your sins have hid his face from you, that he will not hear* (Isaiah 59:1-2).

It is the same today. Many people are crying out to God in vain, simply because of sin in their lives. It may be some sin in the past that has been unconfessed and unjudged, or it may be some sin in the present that is cherished, and very likely not even looked upon as sin; but the sin is there, hidden away somewhere in the heart or in the life, and God *will not hear.*

Anyone who finds his prayers ineffective should not conclude that the thing he asks of God is not according to His will, but he should go alone with God, taking the psalmist's prayer: *Search me, O God, and know my heart; try me and know my thoughts and see if there be any wicked way in me* (Psalm 139:23-24). Then he should wait before God until God points out the thing that is displeasing in His sight. This sin should then be confessed and put away.

I remember a time in my life when I was praying for two definite things that it seemed I must have or God would be dishonored; but the answer didn't come. I woke up in the middle of the night in much physical pain and distress of soul. I cried to God about these things, reasoned with Him as to how necessary it was that I get them and get them at once; but no answer came.

I asked God to show me if there was anything wrong in my own life. Something came to my mind that had often come to it before – something specific but that I was unwilling to confess as sin. I said to God, "If this is wrong, I will give it up." Still no answer came. In my innermost heart, though I had never admitted it, I knew it was wrong.

At last I said, "This is wrong. I have sinned. I will give it up." I found peace. In a few moments, I was sleeping like a child. In the morning, I woke well in body, and the money that was so much needed for the honor of God's name came.

Sin is an awful thing, and one of the most awful things about it is the way it hinders prayer – the way it severs the connection between us and the source of all grace and power and blessing. Anyone who wants to have power in prayer must be merciless in dealing with his own sins. *If I regard iniquity in my heart, the Lord will not hear me* (Psalm 66:18).

As long as we hold on to sin or have any controversy with God, we cannot expect Him to pay attention to our prayers. If there is any sin or dispute that is constantly coming up in your moments of close communion with God, that is the thing that hinders prayer; put it away.

The third hindrance to prayer is found in Ezekiel 14:3: *Son of man, these men have caused their uncleanness to come up over their heart and have established the stumblingblock of their iniquity before their face: should I be enquired of at all by them?* Idols in the heart cause God to refuse to listen to our prayers.

What is an idol? An idol is anything that takes the place of God. It is anything that is the supreme object of our affection. God alone has the right to the supreme place in our hearts. Everything and everyone else must be subordinate to Him.

Many times a man makes an idol of his wife. It is not that a man can love his wife too much, but he can put her in the wrong place. He can put her before God; and when a man regards what his wife wants before what God wants, when he gives her the first place and God the second place, his wife is an idol, and God cannot hear his prayers.

> God alone has the right to the supreme place in our hearts.

A woman often makes an idol of her children. Certainly we cannot love our children too much. The more dearly we love Christ, the more dearly we love our children; but we can put our children in the wrong place. We can put them before God, and we can put their interests before God's interests. When we do this, our children are our idols.

Many people make idols of their reputations or businesses. If you put reputation or business before God, He cannot hear your prayers.

If we really want to have power in prayer, one great question for us to answer is whether God is absolutely first in our lives. Is He before wife or husband, before children, before reputation, before business, before our own lives? If not, prevailing prayer is impossible.

God often calls our attention to the fact that we have an idol in our lives by not answering our prayers, leading us to ask why our prayers are not answered; then we discover the idol, put it away, and God hears our prayers.

The fourth hindrance to prayer is found in Proverbs 21:13: *Whosoever stops his ears at the cry of the poor, he also shall cry himself but shall not be heard.* There is perhaps no greater hindrance to prayer than stinginess – the lack of generosity toward the poor and toward God's work. The person who gives generously to others receives generously from God. *Give, and it shall be given unto you; good measure, pressed down and shaken together and running over, shall men give into your bosom. For with the same measure that ye measure out it shall be measured to you again* (Luke 6:38). The generous man is the mighty man of prayer. The stingy man is the powerless man of prayer.

One of the most wonderful statements about prevailing prayer, which has already been referred to, is 1 John 3:22: *Whatsoever we ask, we receive of him because we keep his commandments and do those things that are pleasing in his sight.* It is made in direct connection with generosity toward the needy. In the context, we are told that it is when we love, not in word or in tongue, but in deed and in truth – when we open our hearts toward the brother in need – then and only then can we have confidence toward God in prayer.

Many men and women who are seeking to find the secret of their powerlessness in prayer do not need to seek far; it is nothing more nor less than downright stinginess. George Müller, to whom reference has already been made, was a mighty man of prayer because he was a mighty giver. What he received from God never stuck to his fingers. He immediately passed it on to others. He was constantly receiving because he was constantly giving.

When one thinks of the selfishness of most churches today, that many churches in this land average very little giving per year per member for foreign missions, it is no wonder that most have so little power in prayer. If we want to get our prayers answered by God, we must give to others. Perhaps the most wonderful **An unforgiving spirit is one of the most common hindrances to prayer.** promise in the Bible in regard to God's supplying our need is Philippians 4:19: *My God shall supply all your need according to his riches in glory by Christ Jesus.* This glorious promise was made to the Philippian church and was made in immediate connection with their generosity.

The fifth hindrance to prayer is found in Mark 11:25: *And when ye are praying, forgive if ye have anything against anyone, so that your Father who is in the heavens will also forgive you your trespasses.* An unforgiving spirit is one of the most common hindrances to prayer. Prayer is answered on the basis that our sins are forgiven; but God cannot deal with us on the basis of forgiveness while we are harboring bitterness or resentment against those who have wronged us. Anyone who is holding on to a grudge against someone else has tightly closed the ear of God against his own prayer.

How many people are crying to God for the conversion of a husband, wife, parent, child, or friend and are wondering why it is that their prayer is not answered, when the whole secret is some grudge they have in their hearts against someone who has hurt them, or whom they think has hurt them. Many mothers and fathers are allowing their children to go down to eternity unsaved, just for the miserable gratification of hating someone.

The sixth hindrance to prayer is found in 1 Peter 3:7: *Ye husbands, dwell with them wisely, giving honour unto the woman, as unto a more fragile vessel and as being heirs together of the grace of life, that your prayers not be hindered.* Here we are plainly told that a wrong relationship between husband and wife is a hindrance to prayer.

In many cases, the prayers of husbands are hindered because of the failure in their duty toward their wives. On the other hand, it is also undoubtedly true that the prayers of wives are hindered because of the failure in their duty toward their husbands. If husbands and wives would diligently seek to find the cause of their unanswered prayers, they would often find the cause to be in their relationship to one another.

Many men make a great show of piety and are very active in Christian work, but show little consideration in how they treat their wives. They are often unkind, if not mean; then they wonder why it is that their prayers are not answered. The verse that we have just quoted explains the seeming mystery. On the other hand, many women who are very devoted to their church and very faithful in attendance treat their husbands with the most unpardonable neglect, are irritable and quarrelsome toward them, wound them by the abrasiveness of their speech and by their angry temper, and then wonder why it is that they have no power in prayer.

There are other things in the relationship between husbands and wives that cannot be spoken of publicly, but which undoubtedly are hindrances in approaching God in prayer. There is much sin covered up under the holy name of marriage that leads to spiritual deadness and powerlessness in prayer. Any men or women whose prayers seem to bring no answer should spread their whole married life out before God and ask Him to put His finger upon anything in it that is displeasing in His sight.

The seventh hindrance to prayer is found in James 1:5-7: *If any of you lacks wisdom, let them ask of God (who gives abundantly to all, and without reproach), and it shall be given them. But ask in faith, not doubting anything. For he that doubts is like the wave of the sea which is driven of the wind and is tossed from one side to another. For let not such a man think that he shall receive anything of the Lord.*

Prayers are hindered by unbelief. God demands that we believe His Word unconditionally and completely. To question it is to make Him a liar. Many of us do that when we plead His promises, and is it any wonder that our prayers are not answered? How many prayers are hindered by our shameful unbelief? We go to God and ask Him for something that is positively promised in His Word, and then we only half expect to get it. *Let not such a man think that he shall receive anything of the Lord.*

Chapter 10

When to Pray

If we want to experience the fullness of blessing available in the prayer life, it is important not only that we pray in the right way, but also that we pray at the right time. Christ's own example is full of suggestions as to the right time for prayer.

In Mark 1:35 we read, *And in the morning, rising up a great while before day, he went out and departed into a solitary place and prayed there.* Jesus chose the early-morning hour for prayer.

Many of the mightiest men of God have followed the Lord's example in this. In the morning hour the mind is fresh and at its very best. It is free from distraction. That absolute concentration upon God that is essential for the most effective prayer is most easily possible in the early-morning hours. Furthermore, when the early hours are spent in prayer, the whole day is sanctified, and power is obtained for overcoming its temptations and for performing its duties.

More can be accomplished in prayer in the first hours of the day than at any other time during the day. Every child of God who wants to make the most out of his life for Christ should set aside the first part of the day to meet God in the study of His Word and in prayer. The first thing we should do each day is go alone with God and face the duties, temptations, and service of that day, getting strength from God for it all. We should get victory before the hour of trial, temptation, or service comes. The secret place of prayer is the place to fight our battles and gain our victories.

The secret place of prayer is the place to fight our battles and gain our victories.

In Luke 6:12 we get further light upon the right time to pray. We read, *It came to pass in those days that he went out into the mountain to pray and continued all night in prayer to God.* Here we see Jesus praying in the night, spending the entire night in prayer. Of course, we have no reason to suppose that this was the constant practice of our Lord, nor do we even know how common this practice was, but there were certainly times when the whole night was spent in prayer. Here too we would do well to follow in the footsteps of the Master.

Certainly there is a way of setting apart nights for

prayer in which there is no benefit, if it is pure legalism; but the abuse of this practice is no reason to neglect it altogether. One should not say, "I'm going to spend a whole night in prayer," with the thought that there is any merit in it that will win God's favor; that is legalism.

We would, though, do well to say, "I'm going to set apart this night for meeting God and obtaining His blessing and power; and if necessary, and if He so leads me, I will give the whole night to prayer." Often we will have prayed things through long before the night has passed, and we can go to bed and find more refreshing and invigorating sleep than if we had not spent the time in prayer. At other times, God will keep us in communion with Himself into the morning hours, and when He does this in His infinite grace, blessed indeed are these hours of night prayer!

Nights of prayer to God are followed by days of power with men. In the night hours the world is hushed in slumber, and we can easily be alone with God and have undisturbed communion with Him. If we set apart the whole night for prayer, there will be no hurry, and there will be time for our own hearts to become quiet before God. There will be time for the whole mind to be brought under the guidance of the Holy Spirit. There will be plenty of time to pray things through. A night of prayer should be put entirely under God's control. We should lay down no rules as to how long we will pray or what we will pray about, but we should be ready to wait upon God for a short time or a long time as He may lead, and to be led out in one direction or another as He sees appropriate.

Jesus Christ prayed before all the critical events in His earthly life. He prayed before choosing the twelve disciples, before the Sermon on the Mount, before starting out on an evangelistic tour, before His anointing with the Holy Spirit and His entrance upon His public ministry, before announcing to the twelve His approaching death, and before the great sacrifice of His life on the cross.

> *And it came to pass in those days that he went out into the mountain to pray and continued all night in prayer to God. And when it was day, he called unto him his disciples; and of them he chose twelve, whom he also named apostles.* (Luke 6:12-13)

> *And it came to pass as he was alone praying, his disciples were with him, and he asked them, saying, Who do the people say that I am? And he straitly charged them and commanded them not to tell anyone this, saying, The Son of man must suffer many things and be rejected of the elders and of the princes of the priests and scribes and be slain and be raised the third day.* (Luke 9:18, 21-22)

Now when all the people were baptized, it came to pass that, Jesus also being baptized and praying, the heaven was opened, and the Holy Spirit descended in a bodily shape like a dove upon him, and a voice came from heaven, which said, Thou art my beloved Son; in thee is my delight. (Luke 3:21-22)

And in the morning, rising up a great while before day, he went out and departed into a solitary place and prayed there. And Simon and those that were with him followed after him. And when they had found him, they said unto him, All men seek for thee. And he said unto them, Let us go into the next towns that I may preach there also, for truly I came forth for that purpose. (Mark 1:35-38)

And he came out and went as he was wont to the mount of Olives, and his disciples also followed him. And when he was at the place, he said unto them, Pray that ye enter not into temptation. And he withdrew from them about a stone's cast and kneeled down and prayed, saying, Father, if thou be willing, remove this cup from me; nevertheless not my will, but thine, be done.

And there appeared an angel unto him from

*heaven, strengthening him. And being in
agony, he prayed more earnestly; and his
sweat was as it were great drops of blood falling down to the ground. And when he rose up
from prayer and was come to his disciples, he
found them sleeping for sorrow and said unto
them, Why sleep ye? rise and pray, lest ye
enter into temptation.* (Luke 22:39-46)

Jesus prepared for every important crisis by a lengthy season of prayer. We should do the same. Whenever any crisis of life is seen to be approaching, we should prepare for it by a time of very definite prayer to God. We should take plenty of time for this prayer.

Christ not only prayed before the great events and victories of His life, but He also prayed after great achievements and important crises. When He had fed the five thousand with the five loaves and two fishes, and the multitude desired to take Him and make Him king, having sent them away, He went up into the mountain alone to pray. He spent hours there alone in prayer to God. So He went on from victory to victory.

*And when he had sent the multitude away,
he went up into a mountain apart to pray;
and when the evening was come, he was
there alone.* (Matthew 14:23)

Jesus therefore knowing that they would

*come and take him by force to make him
king, he departed again into a mountain
himself alone.* (John 6:15)

It is more common for most of us to pray before the great events of life than it is to pray after them, but the latter is just as important as the former. If we would pray after the great achievements of life, we might go on to still greater things. As it is, we are often either feeling important and proud or we are exhausted by the things that we do in the name of the Lord, and so we advance no further. Many men have been endued with power in answer to prayer and have accomplished great things in the

> Jesus Christ gave a special time to prayer when life was unusually busy.

name of the Lord. However, when these great things were accomplished, instead of going alone with God and humbling themselves before Him, giving Him all the glory for what was achieved, they have congratulated themselves for what has been accomplished and have become proud, forcing God to lay them aside. The great things done were not followed by humiliation of self and prayer to God, and so pride came in, and the mighty man lost the power of God.

Jesus Christ gave a special time to prayer when life was unusually busy. He would withdraw at such times from the multitudes that crowded around Him and go into the wilderness and pray. For example, we read in Luke 5:15-16, *But so much the more his fame went forth, and great multitudes came together to hear and to be healed by him of their infirmities. But he withdrew himself into the wilderness and prayed.*

Some people are so busy that they find no time for prayer. Apparently, the busier Christ's life was, the more He prayed. Sometimes He had no time to eat. *And the multitude came together again, so that they could not so much as eat bread* (Mark 3:20). Sometimes He had no time for needed rest and sleep. *And he said unto them, Come ye yourselves apart into a desert place and rest a while; for there were many coming and going, and they had no leisure so much as to eat. And they departed into a desert place by ship privately. And many saw them departing and knew him and ran there afoot out of the cities and arrived before them and came together unto him* (Mark 6:31-33). However, He always took time to pray; and the more work He had, the more He prayed.

Many mighty men of God have learned this secret from Christ, and when the work has increased more than usual, they have set aside an unusual amount of time for prayer. Other men of God, once mighty, have lost their power because they did not learn this secret, and they allowed increasing work to crowd out prayer.

Years ago it was my privilege, along with other theological students, to ask questions of one of the most useful Christian men of the day. I was led to ask, "Will you tell us something of your prayer life?"

The man was silent for a moment, and then, turning his eyes earnestly upon me, replied, "Well, I must admit that I have been so crowded with work of late that I have not given the time I should to prayer."

Is it any wonder that this man lost power, and the great work he was doing was soon noticeably very limited? Let us never forget that the more the work presses on us, the more time we must spend in prayer.

Jesus Christ prayed early in the morning and late at night. He prayed before and after the important events in His life. He prayed when He was especially busy. He also prayed before times of great testing in His life. As He drew nearer and nearer to the cross, and realized that upon that cross He would soon face the great final test of His life, Jesus went out into the garden to pray. He came *unto a place called Gethsemane and said unto the disciples, Sit ye here, while I go and pray yonder* (Matthew 26:36). The victory of Calvary was won that night in the garden of Gethsemane. The calm majesty of His demeanor in meeting the awful onslaughts of Pilate's judgment hall and of Calvary was the outcome of the struggle, agony, and victory of

> Let us never forget that the more the work presses on us, the more time we must spend in prayer.

Gethsemane. While Jesus prayed, the disciples slept; and He stood firm, while they disgracefully fell away.

Many trials come upon us unexpectedly and unannounced, and all that we can do is lift a cry to God for help then and there; but we can see many of life's temptations approaching from the distance, and in such cases the victory should be won before the time of difficulty really reaches us.

First Thessalonians 5:17 says, *Pray without ceasing*, and Ephesians 6:18 says to pray *always with all prayer and supplication in the Spirit*. Our whole life should be a life of prayer. We should walk in constant communion with God. Our souls should be constantly looking up to God. We should walk so habitually in His presence that even when we wake up in the night, it would be the most natural thing in the world for us to speak to God in thanksgiving or in petition.

Chapter 11

The Need of a
General Revival

I f we are to pray properly at such a time as this, much of our prayer should be for a general revival. If there was ever a time in which there was a need to cry unto God, it is now. We should pray in the words of the psalmist: *Wilt thou not* [revive us] *again that thy people may rejoice in thee?* (Psalm 85:6). *It is time for thee, LORD, to work: for they have made void thy law* (Psalm 119:126 KJV).

The voice of the Lord given in the written Word is set aside both by the world and the church. Such a time is not a time for discouragement. The person who believes in God and believes in the Bible can never be discouraged; but it is a time for God Himself to step in and work. The intelligent Christian, the wide-awake watchman on the walls of Zion, may well cry with the psalmist of old, *It is time for thee, LORD, to work: for they have made void thy law* (Psalm 119:126 KJV).

The great need of the day is a general revival. Let us consider first of all what a general revival is. A revival is a time of quickening or of spreading life. God alone can give life, and a revival is a time when God visits His people, imparts new life to them by the power of His Spirit, and through them imparts life to sinners who are dead in trespasses and sins.

We have religious excitement and emotion worked up by the deceptive methods and charming influence of the mere professional evangelist; but these are not revivals, and these are not needed. They are the devil's imitations of a revival. New life from God – that is a revival. A general revival is a time when this new life from God is not confined to scattered localities, but is general throughout the Christian world and the whole earth.

The reason why a general revival is needed is that spiritual famine, desolation, and death are general. They are not confined to any one country, though they may be more conspicuous in some countries than in others. They are found in foreign mission fields as well as in home fields. We have had local revivals. The life-giving Spirit of God has breathed upon certain preachers, churches, and communities; but we desperately need a revival that is widespread and general.

Let us look at the results of a revival. These results are apparent in pastors, in churches, and in the unsaved.

What are some results of a revival in a pastor?

The pastor has a new love for souls. Pastors in general have no such love for souls as they ought to have, no such love for souls as Jesus had, and no such love for souls as Paul had. But when God visits His people, the hearts of pastors are greatly burdened for the unsaved. They go out in great longing for the salvation of their fellow men.

> When true revivals come, pastors get a new love for God's Word and a new faith in God's Word.

They forget their ambition to preach great sermons and to be well known, and they simply desire to see people brought to Christ.

When true revivals come, pastors get a new love for God's Word and a new faith in God's Word. They fling their doubts and criticisms of the Bible to the winds, and they start preaching the Bible – especially Christ crucified. Revivals make pastors who are relaxed in their doctrines strict. A genuine, wide-sweeping revival would do more to turn things upside down and get things right side up than all the heresy trials ever instituted.

Revivals bring to pastors new liberty and power in

preaching. It is no weeklong chore to prepare a sermon, and it is not a nerve-consuming effort to preach it after it has been prepared. Preaching becomes a joy and a refreshment, and there is power in it in times of revival.

The results of a revival on Christians are generally as unmistakable as the results upon the ministry.
In times of revival, Christians come out from the world and live separated lives. Christians who have been lingering in the world, who have been caught up in entertainment, fashion, sports, worldly pleasures, and other foolishness of the world give these things up. These things are found to be incompatible with increasing life and light and holiness.

In times of revival, Christians get a new spirit of prayer. Prayer meetings are no longer a duty, but become the necessity of a hungry, persistent heart. Private prayer is done with new fervor. The voice of earnest prayer to God is heard day and night. People no longer ask, "Does God answer prayer?" They know He does, and they besiege the throne of grace day and night.

In times of revival, Christians go to work for lost souls. They do not go to church services simply to enjoy themselves and be blessed. They go to watch for lost souls and to bring them to Christ. They talk to people on the street and in the stores and in their homes. The cross of Christ, salvation, heaven, and hell become the subjects of constant conversation. Politics, sports, the weather, new clothes, and the latest novels are forgotten.

In times of revival, Christians have new joy in Christ. Life is joy, and new life is new joy. Revival days are joyful days – days of heaven on earth.

In times of revival, Christians get a new love for the Word of God. They want to study it day and night. Revivals are bad for bars and clubs and theaters, but they are good for Christian bookstores and Bible societies.

Revivals also have a clear influence on the unsaved world.

First of all, revivals bring deep conviction of sin. Jesus said that when the Spirit was come, He would convince the world of sin. *Nevertheless I tell you the truth: It is expedient for you that I go away; for if I do not go away, the Comforter will not come unto you; but if I depart, I will send him unto you. And when he is come, he will reprove the world of sin and of righteousness and of judgment* (John 16:7-8). When a revival comes from the Holy Spirit, there is always new conviction of sin. If you see something that people call a revival, and there is no conviction of sin, you can know at once that it is a counterfeit.

Revivals bring conversion and regeneration. When God refreshes His people, He also converts sinners. The first result of Pentecost was new life and power to the 120 disciples in the upper room. The second result was three thousand conversions in a single day. It is always this way. I often hear about revivals in different places where Christians got emotional, but there were no conversions. I have my doubts about that kind of revival. If Christians are truly refreshed, they will go after the unsaved by prayer and testimony and persuasion, and there will be conversions.

Why a general revival is needed.
We see what a general revival is and what it does; let us now see why it is needed now. I think that the mere description of what it is and what it does shows that it is desperately needed, but let us look at some specific conditions that exist today that show the need for it. In showing these conditions, I am likely to be called a pessimist. If facing the facts causes me to be called a pessimist, then I am willing to be called one. If in order to be an optimist one must shut his eyes and call black white, error truth, sin righteousness, and death life, then I don't want to be called an optimist. I am an optimist, though. Pointing out the real condition will lead to a better condition.

Look first at the ministry.
Many who claim to be biblical ministers are practically infidels. That is plain speech, but it is also indisputable fact. There is no essential difference between

the teachings of Thomas Paine and Bob Ingersoll[1] and the teachings of some of our theological professors. The latter are not so blunt and honest about it; they phrase it in more elegant and academic sentences, but it means the same. Much of the so-called new learning and higher criticism is simply a sugarcoated version of Tom Paine's unbelief. Professor Howard Osgood, who is a real scholar and not a mere echo of German biblical criticism, once read a statement of some viewpoints, and he asked if they represented the scholarly criticism of today. When it was agreed that they did, he surprised his audience by saying, "I am reading from Tom Paine's *The Age of Reason.*"

> How many modern pastors know what it is to wrestle in prayer or to spend a good part of a night in prayer?

There is not much new in the higher criticism. Our future ministers are often educated under unbelieving professors, and being impressionable young men when they enter the college or seminary, they naturally come out as infidels in many cases, and then go forth and poison the church.

Even when our ministers are orthodox – as many are, thank God – they are often not men of prayer. How many modern pastors know what it is to wrestle in prayer

---

1   Thomas Paine (1737-1809) was one of America's least-religious Founding Fathers, often considered to be a deist, at best.
Robert Ingersoll (1833-1899) was an American lawyer and politician whose beliefs earned him the nickname "The Great Agnostic."

or to spend a good part of a night in prayer? I do not know how many do, but I do know that many do not.

Many pastors have no love for souls. Not many preach because they feel a deep urgency to preach, or because they feel that people everywhere are perishing, or because by preaching they hope to save some. Not many follow up their preaching as Paul did, by pleading with people everywhere to be reconciled to God.

Perhaps enough has been said about pastors, but it is evident that a revival is needed for their sake, or some of them will have to stand before God overwhelmed with remorse in the terrible day of judgment that is certainly coming.

Look now at the church.

Look at the doctrinal state of the church. It is bad enough. Many do not believe in the whole Bible. They say that the book of Genesis is a myth and that Jonah is an allegory. They even question the miracles of the Son of God. They say that the doctrine of prayer is old-fashioned, and they speak condescendingly of the work of the Holy Spirit. They believe that conversion is unnecessary, and they no longer believe in hell. Look at the trends and errors that have sprung up out of this loss of faith – Christian Science, Unitarianism, Spiritualism, Universalism, metaphysical healing, etc. It is a perfect confusion of doctrines of demons.

Look at the spiritual state of the church. Worldliness

is widespread among church members. Many church members are just as eager as any in the rush to get rich. They use the methods of the world to acquire wealth, and they hold just as tightly to it as anyone.

Prayerlessness abounds among church members on every hand. Christians on average do not spend more than five minutes a day in prayer. Neglect of the Word of God goes hand in hand with neglect of prayer. Many Christians spend twice as much time every day wallowing through the mire of the daily papers as they do bathing in the cleansing water of God's Holy Word. How many Christians average an hour a day spent in Bible study?

Along with neglect of prayer and neglect of the Word of God goes a lack of generosity. The churches are rapidly increasing in wealth, but the treasuries of the missionary societies are empty. Christians do not give much to foreign missions. It is simply appalling.

Then there is the increasing disregard for the Lord's Day. It is fast becoming a day of worldly pleasure instead of a day of holy service. The Sunday newspaper with its empty trivialities and filthy scandals takes the place of the Bible, and traveling, shopping, golf, and exercise take the place of Sunday school, seeking God, and encouraging other Christians in holiness together.

Christians mingle with the world in all forms of questionable amusements. The young man or woman who does not believe in dancing, with its offensive immodesties, the card table with its drift toward gambling, and the theater with its ever-increasing appeal to lust and other sin, is ridiculed as old-fashioned.

How small a proportion of professed Christians have really entered into fellowship with Jesus Christ in His burden for souls! Enough has been said of the spiritual condition of the church.

Now look at the state of the world.

Note how few conversions there are. The Methodist church, which used to lead the way in aggressive evangelistic work and opposition to sin, has actually lost more members than it has gained the last year. Every once in a while we see a church that increases its attendance because people have left other churches, but these are rare exceptions. Even when there are professed conversions, it is not common for the conversions to be deep, thorough, and lasting.

There is lack of conviction of sin. Seldom are people overwhelmed with a sense of their awful guilt in trampling underfoot the Son of God. Sin is regarded as a "misfortune" or an "infirmity," or even as a "mistake," and seldom as an enormous wrong against a holy God.

Unbelief is widespread. Many regard it as a sign of intellectual superiority to reject the Bible, and even to reject faith in God and immortality. It is about the only sign of intellectual superiority that many possess, and that might be the reason they cling to it so tenaciously.

Hand in hand with this widespread infidelity goes blatant immorality, as has always been the case. Infidelity and immorality are conjoined twins. They always exist and grow and spread together. This prevailing immorality is found everywhere.

Look at the legalized adultery that we call divorce. Men marry one wife after another, and are still admitted into good society; and women do likewise. There are thousands of supposedly respectable men in America living with other men's wives, and thousands of supposedly respectable women living with other women's husbands. Even unmarried people are not ashamed to be immoral and live together in sin.

This immorality is found in the theater. The theater at its best is bad enough, but now immorality, immodesty, profanity, and all the unspeakable wicked accompaniments of the stage rule the day, and the women who debase themselves by appearing in such plays are defended in the newspapers and welcomed by supposedly respectable people.

Much of our literature is rotten, but even believers will read books full of sin because they are popular. Art is often a mere covering for shameless indecency. Women are induced to cast modesty to the winds so that the artist may perfect his art and defile his morals.

Greed for money has become a mania with rich and poor. The multi-millionaire will often sell his soul and trample the rights of his fellow men underfoot in the absurd hope of becoming a billionaire, and the working person will often steal, lie, cheat, or do whatever is necessary to increase his wages and power. Wars are waged and men are shot down like dogs to improve commerce and to gain political prestige for unprincipled politicians who parade as statesmen.

The immodesty and immorality of the day lifts its serpent head everywhere. You see it in the newspapers, you see it on billboards, you see it in the advertisements, and you see it everywhere else. You see it on the streets at night. You see it just outside the church door. You find it not only in the awful cesspools set apart for it in the great cities, but it is also crowding farther and farther up our business streets and into the residential portions of our cities. If you look closely enough, you even find it in supposedly respectable homes. Stories of its extent will be carried to your ears by the confessions of brokenhearted men and women. The moral condition of the world in our day is disgusting, sickening, and appalling.

We need a revival that is deep, widespread, general, and in the power of the Holy Spirit. It is a general revival that is needed, or the falling apart of the church, the home, and the state will occur. A revival – new life from God – is the cure. It is the only cure that will stop the awful spread of immorality and unbelief. Mere argument will not do it, but a wind from heaven, a new outpouring of the Holy Spirit, a true God-sent revival will.

Unbelief, biblical criticism, Christian Science, Spiritualism, Universalism, and all false ways will go down before the outpouring of the Spirit of God. It was not discussion, but the breath of God that committed Thomas Paine, Voltaire, Volney,[2] and other infidels to the state of being forgotten. We need a new breath from God to send more men like Elijah, Jonathan Edwards, George Whitefield, and others to preach God's Word in God's power once again in America, England, Wales, Canada, Germany, Ireland, and all over the world. I pray that breath from God comes.

The great need of today is a general revival. The need is clear. It allows no room for difference of opinion. What then shall we do? Pray. Take up the psalmist's prayer that God would revive us again, *that thy people may rejoice in thee* (Psalm 85:6). Take up Ezekiel's prayer: *Come from the four winds, O spirit, and breathe upon these slain, and they shall live* (Ezekiel 37:9). Listen! I hear a noise! Behold a shaking! I can almost feel the breeze upon my cheek. I can almost see the great living army rising to its feet. Shall we not pray and pray and pray and pray until the Spirit comes and God revives His people?

---

2   Francois-Marie Voltaire (1694-1778) is known for his opposition to Christianity and the Bible.
Constantin François de Chassebœuf, comte de Volney (1757-1820) was one of the first modern writers to support the theory that Jesus Christ was a mythical figure.

Chapter 12

The Place of Prayer Before and During Revivals

No treatment of the subject of how to pray would be complete if it did not consider the place of prayer in revivals. The first great revival in Christian history had its origin on the human side in a ten-day prayer meeting. We read of that handful of disciples that they *all continued with one accord in prayer and supplication* (Acts 1:14).

We read of the result of that prayer meeting in Acts 2. *They were all filled with the Holy Spirit and began to speak in other tongues, as the Spirit gave them utterance* (Acts 2:4). Later in the chapter we read that *the same day there were added unto them about three thousand souls* (Acts 2:41). This revival proved to be genuine and permanent. The converts *continued steadfastly in the apostles' doctrine and fellowship and in breaking of bread and in prayers* (Acts 2:42). *And the Lord added to the congregation daily such as should be saved* (Acts 2:47).

Every true revival from that day to this has had its earthly origin in prayer. The great revival under Jonathan Edwards in the eighteenth century began with his famous call to prayer. The marvelous work of grace among the Native Americans under David Brainerd had its origin in the days and nights that Brainerd spent before God in prayer for power from on high for this work.

> **Every true revival from that day to this has had its earthly origin in prayer.**

A most remarkable and widespread display of God's reviving power was that which broke out in Rochester, New York, in 1830, under the labors of Charles G. Finney. It not only spread throughout the state, but ultimately spread to Great Britain as well. Mr. Finney himself attributed the power of this work to the spirit of prayer that prevailed. He describes it in his autobiography in the following words:

When I was on my way to Rochester, as we passed through a village, some thirty miles east of Rochester, a brother minister whom I knew, seeing me on the canalboat, jumped aboard to have a little conversation with me, intending to ride but a little way and return. He, however, became interested in conversation, and upon finding where I was going, he made up his mind to continue and go with me to Rochester.

We had been there but a few days when this minister became so convicted that he could not help weeping aloud at one time as we passed along the street. The Lord gave him a powerful spirit of prayer, and his heart was broken. As he and I prayed together, I was struck with his faith in regard to what the Lord was going to do there. I remember that he would say, "Lord, I do not know how it is; but I seem to know that You are going to do a great work in this city." The spirit of prayer was poured out powerfully, so much so that some people stayed away from the public services to pray, being unable to control their feelings under preaching.

And here I must introduce the name of a man whom I shall have occasion to mention frequently, Mr. Abel Clary. He was the son of a very excellent man, and an elder of the church where I was converted. He was converted in the same revival in which I was. He had been licensed to preach, but his spirit of prayer was such that he was so burdened with the souls of men that he was not able to preach much, but his whole time and strength were spent in prayer. The burden of his soul would frequently be so great that he was unable to stand, and he would twist and turn and groan in agony. I was well acquainted with him and knew something of the wonderful spirit of prayer that was upon him. He was a very silent man, as almost all are who have that powerful spirit of prayer.

The first I knew of his being in Rochester, a gentleman who lived about a mile west of the city called on me one day and asked me if I knew a minister named Mr. Abel Clary. I told him that I knew him well. "Well," he said, "he is at my house, and has been there for some time, and I don't know what to think of him."

I said, "I have not seen him at any of our meetings."

"No," he replied, "he says that he cannot go to the meetings. He prays nearly all the time, day and night, and in such agony of mind that I do not know what to make of it. Sometimes he cannot even remain on his knees, but will lie prostrate on the floor, and groan and pray in a manner that quite astonishes me."

I said to the brother, "I understand it. Please be patient. It will all come out right; he will surely prevail." I knew at the time a considerable number of men who were exercised in the same way.

A Deacon P, of Camden, Oneida County; a Deacon T, of Rodman, Jefferson County; a Deacon B, of Adams, in the same county; this Mr. Clary, and many others among the men, and a large number of women, had this same spirit and spent a great part of their time in prayer. Father Nash, as we called him, who in several of my fields of labor came to me and aided me, was another of those men who had such a powerful spirit of prevailing prayer. This Mr. Clary continued in Rochester as long *as I did, and he did not leave until after I had left. He never, that I could learn, appeared in public, but gave himself wholly to prayer.*

I think it was the second Sunday that I was at Auburn at this time, that I observed in the congregation the solemn face of Mr. Clary. He looked as if he was weighed down with agony of prayer. Being well acquainted with him and knowing the great gift of God that was upon him – the spirit of prayer – I was very glad to see him there. He sat in the pew with his brother, the doctor, who also professed religion, but who had nothing by experience, I would think, of his brother Abel's great power with God.

During a break, as soon as I came down from the pulpit, Mr. Clary, with his brother, met me at the pulpit stairs, and the doctor invited me to go home with him and spend the break with them and have some refreshments. I did so.

After arriving at his house, we were soon called to the dinner table. We gathered around the table, and Dr. Clary turned to his brother and said, "Brother Abel, will you ask the blessing?" Brother Abel bowed his head and began, audibly, to ask a blessing. He had uttered only a sentence or two when he instantly broke down, suddenly moved back from the table, and fled to his room. The doctor supposed he had been taken suddenly ill, and he rose up and followed him. In a few moments he came down and said, "Mr. Finney, Brother Abel wants to see you."

I asked, "What troubles him?"

He answered, "I don't know, but he says that you know. He appears in great distress, but I think it is the condition of his mind."

I understood it in a moment and went to his room. He lay groaning upon the bed, the Spirit making intercession for him and in him, with groanings that could not be uttered. I had barely entered the room, when I heard him say, "Pray, Brother Finney." I knelt down and helped him in prayer by leading his soul out for the conversion of sinners. I continued to pray until his distress passed away, and then I returned to the dinner table.

I understood that this was the voice of God. I saw that the spirit of prayer was upon him. I felt his influence upon me, and I took it for granted that the work would move on powerfully. It did so. The pastor told me afterward that he found that in the six weeks that I was there, five hundred souls had been converted.

Mr. Finney in his *Lectures on Revivals* tells of other remarkable awakenings in answer to the prayers of God's people. He says in one place:

A clergyman in W---n told me of a revival among his people, which began with a zealous and devoted woman in the church. She became concerned about sinners and began praying for them. She prayed, and her distress increased. Finally, she went to her minister, talked with him, and asked him to appoint a meeting for the unsaved to ask about their souls and salvation, for she felt that such a meeting was needed. The minister put her off, for he did not feel the same burden of soul.

The next week she went again and asked him to appoint a meeting. She knew someone would attend, for she felt as if God was going to pour out His Spirit. He put her off again. Finally she said to him, "If you don't appoint a meeting, I will die, for there is certainly going to be a revival." The next Sunday he appointed a meeting and said that if there were any who wished to speak with him about the salvation of their souls, he would meet them on a certain evening. He did not know of anyone who intended to come, but when he went to the place, to his astonishment, he found a large number of concerned inquirers.

In still another place he says:

The first ray of light that broke in upon the midnight which rested on the churches in Oneida County in the fall of 1825, was from a woman in poor health, who, I believe, had never been in a powerful revival. Her soul was concerned about sinners. She was in agony for the land. She did not know what troubled her, but she kept praying more and more, until it seemed as if her agony would destroy her body. At last she became full of joy and exclaimed, "God has come! God has come! There is no mistake about it! The work is begun and is going over all the region!" And sure enough, the work began, her family members were almost all converted, and the work spread all over that part of the country.

The great revival of 1857 in the United States began in prayer and was carried on by prayer more than by anything else. Dr. Cuyler, in an article in a religious newspaper some years ago, wrote the following:

Most revivals have humble beginnings, and the fire starts in a few warm hearts. Never despise the day of small things. During all my own long ministry, nearly every work of grace had a similar beginning. One commenced in a meeting gathered at a few hours' notice in a private house. Another commenced in a group gathered for Bible study by Mr. Moody in our mission chapel. Still another – the most powerful of all – was kindled on a bitter January evening at a meeting of young Christians under my roof. Dr. Spencer, in his Pastor's Sketches (the best book of its kind I have ever read), tells us that a remarkable revival in his church sprang from the fervent prayers of a godly old man who was confined to his room by lameness. That profound Christian, Dr. Thomas H. Skinner, of the Union Theological Seminary, once gave me an account of a remarkable meeting of three devout men in his study when he was the pastor of the Arch Street Church in Philadelphia. They literally wrestled in prayer. They fully confessed their sin and humbled themselves before God. Some church officers came in and joined them. The heaven-kindled flame soon spread through the whole congregation in one of the most powerful revivals ever known in that city.

In the early part of the sixteenth century, there was a great religious awakening in Ulster, Ireland. The lands of the rebel leaders that had been forfeited to the British crown were occupied by a group of colonists who for the most part were governed by a spirit of wild adventure. Real piety was rare. Seven ministers, five from Scotland and two from England, settled in that country, the earliest arrivals settling there in 1613.

It is recorded by someone there at the time that one of these ministers, a man named Blair, "spent many days and nights in prayer, alone and with others, and experienced great closeness with God." Mr. James Glendenning, a man of very limited natural gifts, was a man similarly minded regarding prayer. The work began under Mr. Glendenning.

The historian of the time says, "He was a man who never would have been chosen by a wise assembly of ministers, nor sent to begin a reformation in this land. Yet it was the Lord's choice to use him to begin the admirable work of God which I mention on purpose, so that all may see how the glory is only the Lord's in making a holy nation in this profane land, and that it was *not by might, nor by power, but by my Spirit, said the LORD of the hosts* (Zechariah 4:6)."

In his preaching at Oldstone, multitudes of hearers were very uneasy and felt much terror of conscience. They looked on themselves as altogether lost and condemned. They cried out as in Acts 2:37, "Men and brethren, what shall we do to be saved?" They were stricken with a fit of fainting by the power of God's Word. A dozen in one day were carried out of doors as though dead. These were not women, but some of the boldest spirits of the neighborhood – "some who had formerly feared not with their swords to put a whole market town into a fray." Concerning one of them, the historian writes, "I have heard one of them, then a mighty strong man, but now a mighty Christian, say that his purpose in coming in to church was to consult with his companions about how to cause some mischief."

This work spread throughout the whole country. By the year 1626, a monthly prayer meeting was held in Antrim. The work spread beyond the bounds of Down and Antrim to the churches of the neighboring counties. So great became the religious interest that Christians would come thirty or forty miles to the communions and continue from the time they came until they returned, without growing tired or sleeping. Many of them neither ate nor drank, and yet some of them professed that they "went away most fresh and vigorous, their souls so filled with the sense of God." This revival changed the whole character of Northern Ireland.

Another great awakening in Ireland in 1859 had a somewhat similar beginning. By many who did not know, it was thought that this marvelous work came without warning and preparation, but Reverend William Gibson, the moderator of the General Assembly of the Presbyterian Church in Ireland in 1860, in his very interesting and valuable history of the work, tells how there had been preparation for two years.[3]

There had been constant discussion in the General Assembly about the low state of Christianity and the need for a revival. There had been special sessions for prayer. Finally, four young men, who became leaders in the beginning of the great work, began to meet together in an old schoolhouse in the neighborhood of Kells.

Around the spring of 1858, a work of power began to manifest itself. It spread from town to town and from county to county. The congregations became too large for the buildings, and the meetings were held in the open air, often attended by thousands of people. Many hundreds of people were frequently convicted of sin in a single meeting. In some places, the criminal courts and jails were closed for lack of criminals. There were demonstrations of the Holy Spirit's power in a most

---

3   *The Year of Grace: A History of the Ulster Revival of 1859.*

remarkable way, clearly proving that the Holy Spirit is as ready to work today as in apostolic days, whenever pastors and other Christians really believe in Him and begin to prepare the way by prayer.

Mr. Moody's wonderful work in England, Scotland, and Ireland that afterwards spread to America had its human origin in prayer. Mr. Moody's work did not make much progress until men and women began to cry out to God. Indeed, his going to England at all was in answer to the persistent cries to God by a bedridden saint.

While the spirit of prayer continued, the revival stayed strong; but in time, less and less was made of prayer and the work fell off in power very noticeably. Undoubtedly, one of the great secrets of the weakness, superficiality, and unreality of many of our modern so-called revivals is that more dependence is put upon man's planning than upon God's power. We must seek and obtain this power by earnest, persistent, believing prayer.

> We live in a day characterized by the multiplication of man's methods, while we reject and remain ignorant of God's power.

We live in a day characterized by the multiplication of man's methods, while we reject and remain ignorant of God's power. The great cry of our day is work, work, work – new organizations, new methods, new systems. The great need of our day is prayer. It was a masterstroke of the devil when he got the church so generally to lay aside this mighty weapon of prayer. The devil is perfectly willing that the church would multiply its organizations and cleverly develop methods and plans for the conquest of the world for Christ – as long as it will give up praying.

Satan laughs as he looks at the church today and says to himself, "You can have your Sunday schools and your young people's small groups, your boys' and girls' programs, your vacation Bible schools, your Christian schools, your mega-churches, your retreats, your music programs, your brilliant preachers, and even your revival efforts – as long as you don't bring the power of almighty God into them by earnest, persistent, believing, mighty prayer."

Prayer could produce just as marvelous results today as it ever could – if the church would only get around to fervent, sincere, unceasing, earnest, believing, mighty, God-honoring, biblical prayer. There seems to be increasing signs that Christians are waking up to this fact. Here and there God is laying upon individual pastors and churches a burden for prayer that they have never known before. Less dependence is being put upon methods and more upon dependence upon God. Some pastors are crying out to God day and night for power. Churches and portions of churches are meeting together in the early-morning hours and the late-night hours, crying to God for revival and the power of the Spirit of God.

There is every indication of the coming of a mighty and widespread revival. There is every reason to think that if a revival should occur in any country at this time, it would be more widespread in its extent than any revival in history. We have close and swift communication by travel, by print, and by technology between all parts of the world. A true fire of God kindled in America would soon spread to the uttermost parts of the earth. The only thing needed to bring this fire is prayer.

It is not necessary that the whole church prays to begin with. Great revivals always begin first in the hearts of a few men and women whom God arouses by His Spirit to believe in Him as a living God, as a God who answers prayer, and upon whose heart He lays a burden from which no rest can be found except in persistent crying unto God.

May God use this book to inspire many others to pray that the greatly needed revival may come, and that it would come quickly. May God stir up your own heart to be one of those burdened to pray for true revival until God answers your prayer.

R. A. Torrey –
A Short Biography

R. A. Torrey was an author, conference speaker, pastor, evangelist, Bible college dean, and more. Reuben Archer Torrey was born in Hoboken, New Jersey, on January 28, 1856. He graduated from Yale University in 1875 and from Yale Divinity School in 1878, when he became the pastor of a Congregational church in Garrettsville, Ohio. Torrey married Clara Smith in 1879, with whom he had five children.

In 1882, he went to Germany, where he studied at the universities at Leipzig and Erlangen. Upon returning to the United States, R. A. Torrey pastored in Minneapolis, and was also in charge of the Congregational City Mission Society. In 1889, D. L. Moody called upon Torrey to lead his Chicago Evangelization Society, which later became the Moody Bible Institute. Beginning in 1894, Torrey was also the pastor of the Chicago Avenue

Church, which was later called the Moody Memorial Church. He was a chaplain with the YMCA during the Spanish-American War, and was also a chaplain during World War I.

Torrey traveled all over the world leading evangelistic tours, preaching to the unsaved. It is believed that more than one hundred thousand were saved under his preaching. In 1908, he helped start the Montrose Bible Conference in Pennsylvania, which continues today. He became dean of the Bible Institute of Los Angeles (now Biola University) in 1912, and was the pastor of the Church of the Open Door in Los Angeles from 1915 to 1924.

Torrey continued speaking all over the world and holding Bible conferences. He died in Asheville, North Carolina, on October 26, 1928.

R. A. Torrey was a very active evangelist and soul winner, speaking to people everywhere he went, in public and in private, about their souls, seeking to lead the lost to Jesus. He authored more than forty books, including *How to Bring Men to Christ*, *How to Pray*, *How to Study the Bible for Greatest Profit*, *How to Obtain Fullness of Power in Christian Life and Service*, and *Why God Used D. L. Moody*, and also helped edit the twelve-volume book about the fundamentals of the faith, titled *The Fundamentals*. He was also known as a man of prayer, and his teaching, preaching, writing, and his entire life proved that he walked closely with God.